D0010517

Ancient and Medieval England

Beginnings to 1509

THE HARBRACE HISTORY OF ENGLAND

I   Ancient and Medieval England: Beginnings to 1509
    J. R. Lander
    University of Western Ontario

II Renaissance and Reformation England: 1509–1714
    Charles M. Gray
    University of Chicago

III The Birth and Growth of Industrial England: 1714–1867
    John F. C. Harrison
    University of Sussex

IV England Since 1867: Continuity and Change
    Peter Stansky
    Stanford University

PART I

THE HARBRACE HISTORY OF ENGLAND

J. R. Lander

University of Western Ontario

Ancient and Medieval England

Beginnings to 1509

Under the General Editorship of John Morton Blum

Yale University

Harcourt Brace Jovanovich, Inc.

New York / Chicago / San Francisco / Atlanta

© 1973 by Harcourt Brace Jovanovich, Inc.

All rights reserved. No part of this publication may be reproduced
or transmitted in any form or by any means, electronic or mechanical,
including photocopy, recording, or any information storage and retrieval
system, without permission in writing from the publisher.

ISBN: 0-15-535107-9

Library of Congress Catalog Card Number: 72-97672

Printed in the United States of America

Preface

Many books have been written about medieval England, and a new text may seem superfluous. However, scholarship in this subject, as in so many others today, is rapidly changing; new interpretations have been advanced, in particular about the history of Roman Britain and about later medieval English history. I therefore hope in this volume to present to readers unfamiliar with English history a book that both preserves valuable traditional interpretations that have stood the test of time, and incorporates some of the growing stores of modern knowledge, a great deal of which is still found only in specialized monographs and in the pages of learned journals.

I should like to take this opportunity to thank Professor Donald W. Sutherland of the University of Iowa for his useful suggestions, and Thomas A. Williamson and Dorothy E. Mott of Harcourt Brace Jovanovich for the friendly and helpful way in which they have dealt with the making of this book.

J. R. Lander

Contents

Illustrations

Maps

Ancient and Medieval England

Beginnings to 1509

INTRODUCTION

To understand the social and political institutions of any European country before the late eighteenth or the early nineteenth century, one must first grasp the limitations imposed upon society by the meager resources and primitive techniques of agriculture, transport, building, and manufacturing. One must understand the very small scale of organized life as compared with life today.

Men depended far, far more upon the land than they do in modern industrial societies. Steel for building was unknown; artificial fibers for clothing not yet invented; minerals for transport and, in most areas, for fuel still unutilized. Therefore, the production of timber for construction and heating, of wool and flax for clothing, of hay and oats for horses and oxen—the only means of land transport—severely restricted the acreage for food production. People demanded much more from the land than we do today, yet by modern standards they used it wastefully and unproductively. Although by the thirteenth century some progressive estates used marl and lime, farmyard manure remained the principal fertilizer. Since the manure supply was limited, a large proportion of the arable land—in the more settled communities anything from a third to a half—had to be left fallow each year to recover its fertility. Even the land under crops was far less productive than it is today. Until the late sixteenth century, at the earliest,

The Preindustrial
Way of Life

a bushel of wheat sown returned only about three bushels as compared with twenty nowadays, and an acre of the most fertile land produced only nine or ten bushels of grain as compared with fifty-eight or sixty in England today. Even these low figures are probably unduly flattering to the level of medieval production, for the specific gravity of modern grain is higher and the modern bushel slightly bigger, which may well mean a further increase of more than a fifth.

It is true that the Middle Ages became more advanced in their techniques than the classical world had been. The water mill for grinding grain, though known in the classical world, came into common use only in the Dark Ages.[1] By the twelfth century water power was being applied to industry, to "fulling," one of the finishing processes of the cloth industry, although not to its major and most expensive operations, spinning and weaving. The introduction of the horseshoe and the padded horse collar, probably in the eighth century (the date is extremely controversial), meant a great cheapening of transport. Horses' hooves are particularly susceptible to damp, and their protection by the new iron shoes enabled animals to be worked longer with less fear of deterioration. In classical times horses had

[1] The term generally used to designate the period c. A.D. 500 to c. A.D. 1000.

been harnessed with a yoke in much the same way as oxen. Employed on the horse the yoke could be applied only in such a way that from each end of the yoke two flexible straps encircled the belly and the neck. As soon as the horse began to pull, the neck strap pressed on the jugular vein and windpipe, tending to suffocate him and cut off the flow of blood to the head. The new, rigid padded collar rested on the horse's shoulders, allowing free breathing and circulation. A team of horses in yoke harness could pull a load of only 1,000 pounds or thereabouts; one harnessed with collars could pull four or five times as much.

Even so, the extent of improvements should not be exaggerated. As late as the fifteenth century, the greatest carts could carry no more than a quarter of a ton. Mills were very much at the mercy of nature. In southern Europe they were unusable during the summer months when low rainfall reduced the flow of water in the streams to a mere trickle. In the extreme north and in central Europe they were out of action during the winter months when the rivers were frozen. Even in a more favorable area like England, periodic droughts and floods reduced their utility.

This enforced, involuntary waste of resources dominated agrarian life. Grain production is a highly seasonal occupation. Before the days of intensive mechanization, at least half the man-hours which it demanded were concentrated into a brief period of about eight weeks in the year. When no migrant labor was available to cope with the rush of work at the peak seasons of the agricultural cycle, particularly the harvest, the peasant and the laborer were only partially occupied during most of the year. Even with the high crop yields and high degree of mechanization of the twentieth century, the wages of agricultural workers are lower than those of industrial workers. All through the medieval and early modern world, nine-tenths of the population were peasants or laborers wringing their poor subsistence directly from the low yield of the soil. That yield was so low that even at the end of the sixteenth century, miserably paid as he was, the wages of a single laborer were almost prohibitive for the owner of a sixty-acre farm.

Moreover, the medieval life-pattern made for low productivity. The popular idea that large families were common in the preindustrial world seems baseless. Although many of the aristocracy, for dynastic reasons, married early, peasants, artisans, and merchants married much later than nineteenth-century factory workers or twentieth-century students. Peasants often had to wait to marry until they inherited the family holding; artisans and merchants served long apprenticeships. Child mortality was appallingly high, and the expectation of life, even for those who survived their middle twenties, was probably well under fifty. The combination of late marriage and low expectation of life kept down the number of children to about four or five per marriage.

In addition, the population was less fitted to bear the burden of life than it is in industrial societies today. Physical deterioration came far earlier than it comes to most people in the mid-twentieth century. Most men and women suffered chronic bad health by the age of forty. As in underdeveloped countries today, probably only a minority of people came to maturity with both parents still living. Two-fifths of the population were children under fourteen, as compared with about a quarter in England today. Such a population, with so short a life span and so short a maximum capacity for work, must have been terribly unproductive by modern standards. In 1960 in the United States, every farm worker produced enough food to feed twelve people. The figure for medieval and early modern England was probably nearer to that for contemporary Ghana, where a single worker on the land can still feed no more than one and a half persons. At the end of the seventeenth century, with three-quarters of its present-day acreage under the plow, England could feed a population of only an eighth its present size, and even then nearly half the national income was spent on food—including a seventh on beer alone.

It is often claimed that the masses lived in bitter poverty because lay landlords, great and small, who made up about 2 percent of the population, and the Church took an undue proportion of their tenants' produce in services and rents. But too much should not be made of this claim in any discussion of poverty. Throughout most of the Middle Ages the techniques of estate management were no higher than those of production, and it was no easy matter to collect fully even a lord's legally recognized dues. Endemic violence and disorder in the earlier centuries were as vital as the landlords' exactions in holding down the peasants' standards. But the main causes of almost unbelievably low living standards were the wide reliance on man's almost unaided physical strength and the primitive techniques which were all the preindustrial world commanded. No matter what social and political relations there were, or could have been, given the means of production available, the standard of life for the great majority of people could have been no other than low. Until very recent times no society, whatever the distribution of wealth between its different classes, has ever been capable of providing a high material standard of life for more than a tiny minority of its population.

Social organization functioned on a very small scale. The most plausible guess at the population of Roman Britain is about one million. By the time of the Norman Conquest it was possibly greater by another hundred thousand or slightly more—just under double the population of New Orleans or about two-thirds of that of Detroit in 1960. In the early fourteenth century it reached a peak of 3.75 million or thereabouts—about 8 or 9 percent higher than the population of Chicago today. By the 1390s the Black Death and subsequent, scarcely less lethal, outbreaks of plague had reduced it possibly by two-fifths. It began to rise again, rather slowly from about the 1430s, more rapidly from the 1460s, until by 1650 it was about 5.1 million—still half a million less than the combined population of Manhattan, Brooklyn, and the Bronx.

Villages in the late fourteenth century varied from about 50 to 150 people, depending on the nature of the land. A large number lay in the range of 80 to 120 inhabitants. London, by far the largest city in the country, had possibly reached 35,000 (about the size of Beverley, Massachusetts) in 1400. It may have reached 50,000 a century later. At the beginning of the sixteenth century about twenty provincial towns boasted more than 3,000 people, and only a few, like Bristol, Norwich, York, and Coventry, passed the 4,000 mark. Princeton, New Jersey, with over 11,800 people, would have been regarded as a giant in those days. By modern standards, or even by the standards of fifteenth-century Italy, most late-medieval English towns were little more than prosperous villages. Market towns could vary from as few as 200 or 300 people to as many as 1,000— or 2,000—if they were county towns or the sites of great churches. In 1545 a chantry certificate described Oakham, the county town of Rutland, as "a great town," though its inhabitants numbered little more than 500. Agriculture was still Oakham's main occupation; its atmosphere was still predominantly rural. Craftsmen and artisans made up at most a quarter of its population. Many of these townsmen farmed and could be, and were, indifferently described as craftsmen, yeomen, or husbandmen. Many of Oakham's so-called artisans were only part-time craftsmen who often put up their shutters and went out to work on their farms. Except for a few places running a specialized trade in grain or cloth, most country towns, though somewhat bigger, were of very much the same type as Oakham: minute local centers of trade for villages within a radius of six to twelve miles.

Life in such communities had an intensely personal flavor, quite unlike that of modern cities. People lived where they worked, and everything, even in London, took place within comparatively easy walking distance. The priest knew intimately every inhabitant of his parish. The rich—the "maiores," as they were called in town records and chronicles—in spite of hot-tempered personal rivalries amongst themselves, more or less ruled the towns in their own interest, controlled trade, and meted out discipline and charity to the poor. These were tight, hierarchical societies, with the tight control and discipline which generally permeate social groups small enough for the existence and conduct of their inhabitants to be the concern of almost everyone.

Life, too, was much more regional in flavor, and fluctuated much more violently over the seasons and over the years than it does today. Perhaps of all historical differences these are the most difficult to grasp in a generation for which the development of cheap, rapid transport has ironed out the regional and even, to some extent, the seasonal variations of life. A line drawn roughly from the Severn to the Humber divides England into a high-land and a lowland zone. To the north and west, mountains and moors dominate the terrain, a land of poor, thin soils and heavy rainfall suitable mainly for animal production. The richer soils and drier climate of the south and east are as suitable for grain as for grass and allow a wider choice of crops. Even within these main divisions, however, wide differences in both farming and social structure sprang from geological and geographi-cal variations. John Leland (d. 1552) described northern Warwickshire, the district known as Arden, as "much enclosed, plentiful of grass, but no great plenty of corn." It was indeed a district with a predominance of grazing over arable land. Only a few miles to the south "Fielden" Warwickshire lay unenclosed, producing large quantities of grain. The composition of their populations differed remarkably: half the population of Arden were free tenants—freedom went with forest conditions; two-thirds of the people of the "Fielden" area were villeins.

Differences should not, however, be pressed too far, for difficulties of transport made specialization impossible beyond a certain point. Even in the mid-sixteenth century the transport of wheat from the Oxford area to London, a mere fifty miles, added 50 percent to its price. It was, therefore, imperative to produce all types of food locally. Thus, the composition of people's diets varied widely in different areas and in different seasons. By spring supplies were invariably low and had become almost unbearably monotonous, as well as high in price for those who did not grow their own. The weather could play havoc with prices: the cost of food was always considerably higher in winter than in the summer and the fall. As late as the mid-nineteenth century Thomas Hardy described in *The Mayor of Caster-bridge* how a poor harvest could ruin the quality of the people's bread during the following year, and, indeed, the plot of the novel depends on wild speculation about the yield of the approaching harvest during a late summer of highly uncertain weather.

During the Middle Ages and later, starvation was an ever-present threat. Torrential rains over three consecutive years in the second decade of the fourteenth century produced disastrous harvests and afflicted fright-ful famine on the peoples of Europe. According to the *Annals of Bermond-sey*, the poor ate cats, dogs, the dung of doves, even their own children. Another chronicler, John Trokelowe, relates that starving men and women haunted the London streets, that filthy corpses lay everywhere in the lanes, that famished thieves in the jails ferociously fell on new prisoners and devoured them half alive.

Nor did the pangs of scarcity end with the Middle Ages. In the early seventeenth century Sir William Pelham of Broklesby in north Lincolnshire wrote to a friend of the frightful dearth that afflicted his own estates:

There are many thousands in these parts who have sold all they have even to their bed straw and cannot get work to earn any money. Dog's flesh is a dainty dish, and found upon search in many houses, also such horse flesh as hath lain long in a deke [ditch] for hounds. And the other day one stole a sheep who for mere hunger tore a leg out and did eat it raw. All that is most certain true and yet the great time of scarcity is yet to come.[2]

It may well be that the years between 1620 and 1650 saw the most frightful suffering that the masses of Englishmen had known since the early fourteenth century and, for the same reason, an increase in population, for which the still medieval system of agriculture could not provide. Only in the late seventeenth century did agricultural improvements finally banish the grisly specter of famine. Even then, three-fifths of the population were always potentially destitute (some were destitute from birth to death) in that they always lived so near the margin of survival that they had nothing to fall back on in times of crisis, such as a bad harvest or a sharp rise in prices. Short of the horrible involuntary remedy of the destruction of a large part of the population by plague, there was no exit from this vicious circle of excessive reproduction followed by privation, until cheap transport made possible the import of food on a large scale and industrialization created new wealth to pay for it. Until then, life for the majority of the population, as Thomas Hobbes averred, was and could be no other than "nasty, brutish, and short."

[2] Quoted in J. Thirsk, *English Peasant Farming* (London, 1957), p. 192.

CHAPTER ONE

Between about 2500 B.C. and the Roman occupation (A.D. 43), a succession of peoples from the European mainland invaded Britain. Their ships were tiny, so these immigrations were small in scale, resulting in a slow, gradual penetration of the land rather than an "occupation," as that word is generally understood. The first cultivators of the soil came from Spain to occupy the western part of the islands, scattering over parts of the Scottish Highlands, Ireland, the Isle of Man, Wales, and southwestern England, where, particularly in southwestern England, they have left their cairns and long barrows, the great communal stone graves of their tribal culture. Somewhat later, other wanderers came in from the east, and between about 1500 and 1000 B.C., reinforced by more immigrants, they coalesced to form a fairly rich and peaceful Celtic society with its own distinctive culture: a society of farmers and traders who, at some unknown date, abandoned the use of finely worked flint tools and weapons in favor of bronze instruments made from Irish copper and Cornish tin. This civilization was a local variation of a European-wide Celtic culture that takes its name from the village of La Tène on Lake Neuchâtel in Switzerland. Although by later standards their life was primitive, the Celts achieved a consummate mastery in the design and craftsmanship of bronze handmirrors, brooches, bracelets, necklaces, helmets, and harness fittings.

Roman Britain

About the fifth century B.C. the transition from the Bronze to the Iron Age began in Britain. Over about 400 years still more immigrants invaded the country from areas as widely separated as Brittany in the west and the mouths of the Rhine in the north and east. These new tribes, of partly Celtic, partly Teutonic descent, seem to have been far more aggressive than their predecessors of the Bronze Age, competing for territory as they migrated in much the same way as the Anglo-Saxon tribes later fought among themselves in the sixth and seventh centuries A.D. By the time Julius Caesar had conquered most of Gaul (56 B.C.) these successive invasions had produced in various parts of Britain a wide diversity of cultures—varying from Neolithic through Bronze Age to Iron Age. There was not, nor was there to be for centuries, any standardization of culture and institutions.

The Roman Invasions

Many of these later Iron Age invaders were tied by kinship and common interest with the tribes of Gaul. The Parisi, for example, who lived in what is now the East Riding of Yorkshire, were related to those who gave their name to the capital of France. By this time the economic center of Britain

Interior of stone hut, over 3,000 years old, from Neolithic village at Skara Brae in the Orkney Islands, Scotland. (Edwin Smith.)

had shifted from the southwest to the southeast, where tribes like the Belgae and the Cantuvellauni, because of their continental connections, became something of a menace to the stability of Roman Gaul. British tribes might incite rebellion against the Roman authorities there or give refuge to potentially dangerous exiles. Finally, the large degree of common interest between the tribes on each side of the English Channel drove the Emperor Claudius in A.D. 43 to conquer Britain, in order to complete and stabilize his northern lines of defense. It may well have seemed safer to conquer Britain than to maintain a large army in Gaul as a safeguard against insurrections encouraged or promoted from the nearby island.

La Tène art: The Desborough mirror; height, 13 ¾". (Courtesy of the British Museum.)

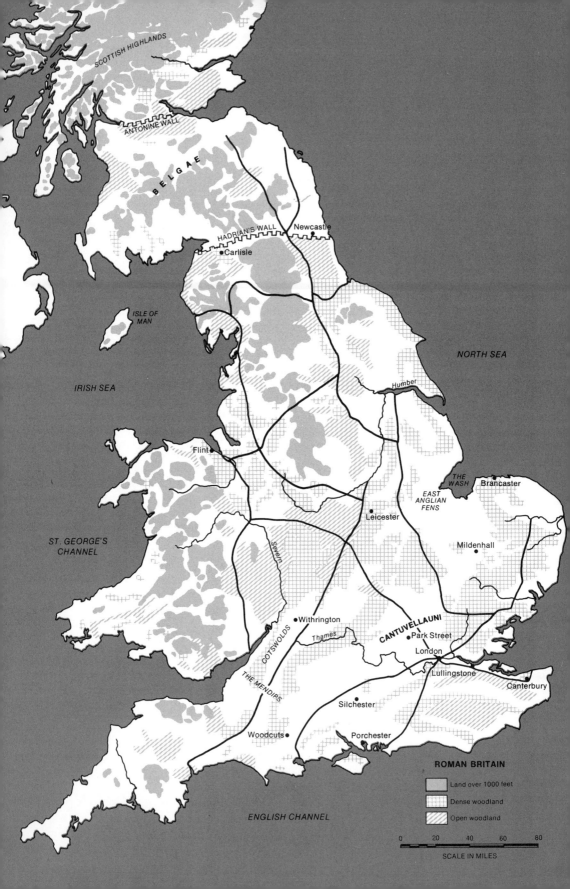

SCOTTISH HIGHLANDS

ANTONINE WALL

BELGAE

HADRIAN'S WALL ● Newcastle

● Carlisle

ISLE OF MAN

IRISH SEA

NORTH SEA

● Flint

THE WASH

Humber

EAST ANGLIAN FENS

● Brancaster

ST. GEORGE'S CHANNEL

● Leicester

● Mildenhall

Severn

● Withrington

Thames

CANTUVELLAUNI

● Park Street

COTSWOLDS

London

● Lullingstone

THE MENDIPS

● Canterbury

● Silchester

● Woodcuts

● Porchester

ROMAN BRITAIN

Land over 1000 feet

Dense woodland

Open woodland

ENGLISH CHANNEL

0   20   40   60   80

SCALE IN MILES

Map of Roman Britain. (Adapted from Collingwood and Myres, *Roman Britain and the English Settlements*, Clarendon Press, Oxford.)

Such a course may also have brought distinct economic advantages to Rome. The Belgae, who had gained control of southeast Britain about 75 B.C., together with other related tribes, possessing more iron tools than earlier settlers (in particular, plows with longer, wider iron shares), were able to clear and exploit the heavier and richer soils of the valleys, which yielded more abundant crops than the upland areas to which primitive implements had hitherto restricted arable cultivation. Thus they were able to produce considerable grain crops for export. Expectation of mineral wealth may also have been immensely attractive to the Romans. They certainly knew of the tin deposits in the southwest and the iron ore seams of the southeast, and they may even have been aware that there was lead to exploit in the Mendips. Judging from the speed with which they began to exploit British mines, they must have known something of the country's wealth in mineral deposits before they arrived there. We have a Roman lead ingot from the Mendips dated A.D. 49, only six years after the Claudian invasion, and another from Flintshire of A.D. 74.

Once conquered, the country was more or less divided following two natural zones, the highland and the lowland, by a line running northeast from the Severn to the Humber. The northern highland zone was, roughly speaking, an area of military government; the southern lowland zone, an area of civil government. To protect and develop lowland Britain and to make certain of the security of Gaul (which after all had been one of the purposes of the invasion), the Romans pushed north to establish a strong frontier.

Hadrian's Wall

When the Emperor Trajan died in A.D. 117, Roman expansion came to an end, and it was the lifework of his successor, Hadrian, to construct efficient, permanent boundary lines against the barbarians in many parts of the empire. Hadrian, by this time one of the most experienced military engineers and architects of the day, went to Britain in A.D. 122 as part of a tour of inspection of the western provinces and ordered the building, carried out between A.D. 122 and 133, of the great wall stretching for seventy miles across the Tyne gap from Newcastle in the east to some four miles west of Carlisle. The wall not only defended the small province of Britain; Hadrian planned it as the extreme northwestern section of a series of frontier defenses flung out across Europe from the Black Sea to the mouths of the Rhine. The effort that went into this immense and costly rampart shows how vital Hadrian considered the need for defense at this point. Whereas long stretches of the new German frontier consisted merely of a wooden palisade, Hadrian's Wall was an immense stone rampart, originally from eight to ten feet thick and possibly sixteen feet high, with mile-castles and signal turrets regularly spaced along it. Apart from the earth and the rubble thrown up to form its core, it has been calculated that well over a million cubic feet of stone had to be quarried for the wall and shaped into twenty-five million blocks of ashlar for its facings.

The western section of the wall was originally built of turf and replaced by stone some years later. Kipling, with considerable historical imagination, made his Roman officer say:

> Just when you think you are at the world's end, you see a smoke from East to West as far as the eye can turn, and then, under it, also as far as the eye can stretch, houses and temples, shops and theatres; barracks and granaries, trickling along like lice behind it—always behind—one long, low rising and falling, and hiding and showing of towers. And that is the wall. . . . Old men who have followed the Eagles since boyhood say nothing in the Empire is more wonderful than the first sight of the wall.[1]

In spite of its solidity, Hadrian thought of the wall as a political rather than primarily a military barrier. It was not a rampart to be defended like a city wall. The inhabitants of the Pennines to the south remained hostile to Rome until as late as the first years of the third century, and for that reason a great earthwork to the south of the wall completed the defensive system. With a hostile population on both sides, the wall provided an immense observation platform which enabled its garrison to detect and control the movements of the tribes to the north and south.

Magnificent as it was, the wall was probably less successful a barrier than Hadrian had hoped it would be. Possibly, the cost of maintenance and garrisons proved heavier than he had expected. At its maximum, the garrison was 9,500 men. About A.D. 142 the Romans pushed their frontier northward again, establishing the much less impressive, much less solidly constructed Antonine Wall, stretching for only thirty-seven miles across the Forth-Clyde isthmus. This, in turn, failed to bring stability to the frontier area, and after a mere decade the troops fell back to the Hadrianic line.

Imperative need forced the Romans to devote immense resources to defense, for, after all, the northern wall was only a small part of a great interlocking, imperial defense system. To thwart potential disloyalty in the tribes' home regions, Rome recruited its subject tribesmen to serve in distant

---

[1] Rudyard Kipling, *Puck of Pook's Hill* (1905), pp. 140–41.

Hadrian's Wall, showing a surviving segment, built *c.* A.D. 120. (J. Allan Cash—Rapho-Guillumette.)

provinces. A British regiment guarded the Danube frontier in Pannonia while Syrian archers manned Hadrian's Wall and a Spanish regiment was stationed on the Antonine Wall. This ever-urgent defense problem was never satisfactorily resolved, and all through the Roman occupation Britain continued to be a frontier province from which military activity was rarely absent. Defense was also immensely costly, for possibly as many as one in ten of the adult male population was permanently in the legions and auxiliary regiments, an immense proportion for the rest to feed, considering the low productivity of contemporary agriculture. Although the needs of the garrisons stimulated trade and the growth of a merchant class, the taxation required to maintain the defenses certainly depressed the subjected peasantry. But the wall, at least for many years, gave security and peace to the lowland zone.

Patterns of Settlement: Economic Life and Provincial Culture

Britain was one of the imperial provinces, that is, a province under the direct control of the emperors themselves. The Romans, with their vast experience of government, were able, within a single generation of the Claudian invasion of A.D. 43, to impose a degree of organization and unity which the Anglo-Saxons achieved only after 500 years of settlement. Unfortunately, however, as our knowledge of Roman Britain grows, the outlines of its development, which, to a former generation of historians, seemed to be reasonably well-defined, have become much more complex, not to say blurred, and even somewhat confusing. Some years ago it was more or less orthodox to write of a triad of towns, villas, and villages: the towns being an attempt to civilize the richer class of the native population to Mediterranean urban values, an attempt overambitious, both culturally and economically, which began to fail in the third century and totally collapsed during the fourth; the villas a combination of great farms and gentlemen's residences in the countryside being a more successful, and more enduring, auxiliary to the attempt; and the villages, groups of primitive huts whose inhabitants Roman civilization hardly touched. All these concepts have been greatly modified by recent archaeological evidence. There are now known to have been many more towns than historians had once thought, although many were minute, no more than walled villages straggling along some main road. The decline of the greater centers is placed considerably later, not until the end of the fourth century. Most villas were far from being the luxurious dwellings of tradition, and individual farms rather than villages may have housed most of the peasantry.

After the first twenty or thirty years of purely military occupation, the Roman government began to organize the lowland zone into cantons on the basis of the existing tribes, each with its own capital and senate to act as a focus of loyalty for the British aristocracy. According to his son-in-law Tacitus, Agricola, who governed the province from A.D. 78 to 84, partly paid with public money for the building of these new towns to seduce the provincials from their warlike habits to the delights of a Latin, urban culture.

The greater towns were laid out in the typical Roman manner: on a grid system with the streets intersecting at right angles and dividing the whole area into *insulae,* or rectangular sections. Progress towards anything like Mediterranean standards of splendor was somewhat slow. Even as late as A.D. 130, most buildings in London were still half-timbered structures of clay and wood; mosaics first appeared in Canterbury only about twenty years later. It was not until the first half of the second century that masonry began to replace these more primitive early buildings, but from then on the greater towns excelled anything that England was to know again for centuries. At Silchester, for example, there was a forum containing shops and government offices surrounded by a colonnade with pillars of Bath stone. One side was occupied by a great public hall or basilica,[2] over 230

---

[2] At this time, "basilica" denoted a secular building, not a church.

feet long and nearly 60 feet wide, divided into a central nave and two side aisles, parts of it lavishly decorated with both Purbeck and imported Italian marbles.

There may have been, at various times, as many as 700 villas in Roman Britain, although not all of them were occupied at once or continuously through the whole period. Although the most northerly was not far from Durham, most of them lay in the lowland zone south of the Humber and east of the Severn. As noted earlier, Agricola wished to transform the aristocracy into townsmen; such people were unlikely to build villas as well as townhouses. The villas erected during the first and second centuries were less the homes of the rich than those of their tenants, younger sons, and other relations. Their homes were modest bungalows containing from six to ten rooms, decent farmhouses rather than the well-appointed mansions commonly associated with the words "Roman villa."

Such a villa at Park Street in Hertfordshire was built to replace a Belgic farm that had been made entirely of timber. About A.D. 65 its owners built a new house with a lower storey of flints set in mortar with brick quoins. Its upper storeys were still timber. Although it had only five rooms and a cellar, the new house covered more than four times the area of its predecessor. As it contained glazed windows, interior walls decorated with highly colored plaster, and Purbeck and Sussex marble fittings, it was far more comfortable than anything that its inhabitants had formerly known. With the general growth in prosperity during the next century and a half, the owners of Park Street, like many others, once again rebuilt (c. A.D. 150) to a higher standard. Even then, however, their home remained a Roman farmhouse rather than a luxurious establishment: it had no bathhouse (one of the main symbols of Roman luxury), only the simplest and plainest mosaic floors, and its hypocaust, or hot-air heating system, was more likely to have been used for drying grain than for heating the rooms in which the family lived.

Only a small number of Roman villas in Britain, about seventy-five, were luxurious mansions. All these were built late; none, apparently, before the fourth century. The reasons for their comparatively sudden development are still something of a mystery. Some writers think that the greater aristocracy moved out of the towns at this time, but something of a revival of town life after a slight depression during the third century suggests that they now, for the first time, maintained both town and country establishments. Villas of this type, like the one at Lullingstone in Kent, spread over thirty to fifty rooms, with fine mosaics, bathhouses, elaborate heating systems, and luxurious appointments. The tiny minority of the population which inhabited them enjoyed a more comfortable life than anything known again before the great country houses of the eighteenth century.

Although the Romans improved drainage and built roads and canals by forced labor, the inhabitants of the farms and villages[3] were affected only in the most superficial way by the new culture. For example, although the inhabitants of a farm like Woodcuts in Cranborne Chase bought bronze implements of a Roman type—box fittings, knife handles, and intaglio rings—they lived in the simplest huts of clay and thatch and farmed very much as they had always done. They may, indeed, have been much worse off than before the Romans arrived, for the government requisitioned as much as one-half to three-fifths of their total grain crops. Two areas in

[3] An earlier generation of archaeologists exaggerated the number of villages in many areas because they mistook the accumulated debris of several generations on isolated farm sites as evidence of village life.

Mosaic pavement from a Roman villa at Fishbourne, Sussex. (Copyright Sussex Archaeological Trust.)

particular, the East Anglian Fens and the Wessex Chalklands—judging from the total absence there of towns, villas, and all the more sophisticated forms of life—may well have been vast imperial estates, organized to meet the needs of the armies stationed in the highland zone, the grain of the Fenland going to the north, that of the western area to Wales. The slaves of the imperial estates and the peasants of other districts like Woodcuts knew little of the advantages of civilization available to those in the new Roman towns.

Britain's economy was even more overwhelmingly rural than that of most lands of the classical world. The majority of the population—the owners of the great estates, the occupants of the modest villas, the peasants, the slaves of the imperial domains—produced grain, wool, and cattle. Some grain was exported to the Rhine area in the fourth century, but it is doubtful whether the immense demands of the armies stationed in the country (the surplus production of at least two or three peasants was needed to feed one soldier) could have left any considerable surplus to be sold abroad. In addition, the military demand for leather, clothing, shield-coverings, and tents (the Latin for "under canvas" is *sub pellibus*) was almost insatiable. Cloth production for export, particularly in the Cotswolds, was already famous, as it continued to be in Anglo-Saxon times. Although the Romans may have been disappointed in their expectations of mining gold, Britain became a valuable source of iron, lead, and the silver that could be extracted from lead ores. Tin and copper mining was profitable until competition from Spanish mines forced its decline. The production of coarse pottery for domestic use became an important industry, although attempts to produce the more refined types of red Samian ware were far from being a commercial success. Pottery was also imported from the Rhine area, fine glass from Alexandria and Syria, later from Cologne and Normandy. Luxury goods and wine met the demands of the well-to-do. All in all, however, we know far too little about the country's economy to hazard even a guess about the extent or value of its commerce.

Four hundred years is a very long time, nearly as long as the period between the first European settlements in America and the present day. The province did not, of course, remain in the same condition during the entire Roman occupation; above all, it was a society that bent and changed under the immense burden and changing needs of defense. The Roman Empire had ceased its long and profitable period of expansion by the time of the Emperor Hadrian (A.D. 117–38). Much of its wealth had always been predatory—the loot of conquest and the exploitation of newly conquered territories—and Britain itself had been looted and exploited in the early days of occupation. Seneca (4 B.C.–A.D. 65), for example, supported his philosophical studies by extensive usury. He is said, at one point, to have had ten million sesterces out on loan in Britain, and he can hardly have been the only Roman money-lender operating in the province. Loans of this kind undoubtedly supported the city-building programs from Agricola's time onward, when a great deal of money was spent on the amenities of town life— marketplaces, temples, baths, and the like. With the end of expansion the empire was never at peace: it continually faced internal disorder and the threat of attack from without. By the end of the second century the wall and the forts of the highland zone were insufficient for defense, and urban expenditure had to be switched to fortifications—probably at first as a protection against internal disorder and attacks from the north of Hadrian's Wall. The Roman towns had originally been open towns. Toward the end of the second century many of them, even the smaller ones no bigger than mere villages, were first enclosed by turf ramparts, which were later, some time during the third century, faced with masonry.

The Barbarian Invasions

The third century, when waves of barbarians swept across the continental provinces of the empire, was a time of comparative prosperity for Britain. In its northern isolation it was spared the chaos and misery which the invaders inflicted almost everywhere else. At the same time, it did not entirely escape the new growing menace that everywhere threatened the empire. As four centuries later the country's wealth attracted the Vikings, it now lured Saxon pirates from Frisia and the Rhineland. The threat had begun earlier, but from about 262 to 280 these pirates became a terrible menace to the population of the eastern coast, which, as the Roman troops and fortifications were mainly in the north and west, lay almost completely open to any boat able to cross the North Sea. To meet the new menace, the government devised a system of coastal forts from Brancaster, just outside the Wash, to Porchester, near Portsmouth on the southern coast. These new forts gave some protection to the east and southeast. This protection, however, was limited. Rome had always based its military organization on highly trained infantrymen. Dominated by this tradition, the government now seemed incapable of developing an efficient naval organization with swift patrol vessels and large enough battle fleets to control the North Sea and the English Channel.

During the fourth century Britain, unlike most other provinces, was still prosperous. Indeed, its civilization and prosperity had never been higher than in these years. At the same time it existed in increasingly hostile surroundings, and its security, due in part to government decisions beyond local control, became more and more tenuous. Hadrian's Wall could generally keep out the tribes from the north, and many towns yet again improved their defenses by adding bastions to their third-century walls to guard against the increasing risk of attack by roving bands of desperadoes. Yet, because of the inadequate naval organization, the province could survive the Saxon raids only as long as these were made by small independent bands acting in isolation, seeking merely plunder, not a permanent settlement in the country.

In 367 the barbarians conspired for the first time. A combined raid of Picts from the distant north, Scots from Ireland, and Saxon pirates, who also raided the coasts of Gaul, produced appalling disasters and devastations—but the damage was only temporary, and recovery seems to have been remarkably swift. The defenders rebuilt Hadrian's Wall for the last time (this work is notably inferior to earlier reconstructions), but thereafter we know little of it. Probably, the government now abandoned the traditional organization of garrisons in favor of the creation, or recognition, of

Neptune dish from the Mildenhall treasure; approx. 23". (Courtesy of the British Museum.)

British buffer states capable of defending themselves against external attack on either side. In the last resort, however, the province went under because it depended for its defense on the will of emperors, whose main interests lay elsewhere. Between 383 and 407 the emperors repeatedly withdrew the island's garrisons to deal with military crises elsewhere in Europe.

The so-called withdrawal of the legions in 410 is an exceedingly misleading concept. Almost all the effective troops had long ago been withdrawn to Italy or Gaul. It would probably be more accurate to say that the Emperor Honorius now advised private citizens to take up arms in their own defense, a course hitherto strictly forbidden. Honorius and his advisers may have regarded this measure of self-defense as no more than a temporary expedient to meet a critical situation on the Continent, and many of the Roman provincials may have regarded the troubles through which they were passing as no more than a temporary cloud over their still prosperous and civilized way of life. In this they were mistaken, and from now on conditions grew inexorably, if gradually, worse. Deprived of the guidance and organization of the central government, the Romano-British failed in the end to sustain their own defense.[4] As their way of life deteriorated, some of the rich undoubtedly fled, burying their family silver in the hope of returning in better days: the famous Mildenhall treasure, a splendid service of domestic silver, was only the most magnificent of such burials. The better days they expected never returned. For the majority who remained in the country, the use of money declined: they had to meet their needs increasingly by barter. Transport between villa and town grew increasingly insecure. Slaves escaped and thus destroyed the foundation of the villa economy. A few of the villas were sacked by invaders and native marauders; most suffered a long drawn-out decay. The towns, in some form at least, probably survived longer. Even after trade decayed, they would still have been useful as strong points as long as their surrounding regions could be cultivated. But as the economy inexorably declined, the maintenance of even recent buildings must have become more and more difficult There was probably very little survival of organized life after the year 500.

Life in Roman Britain about 400, though its base was already highly precarious, was as prosperous and as civilized as it had ever been. A century later it was fragmented, tribal, and, although the southwest in particular still maintained contact with the rest of Europe and even imported some of its luxury goods, completely sub-Roman.

Effects of the Roman Occupation

The effects of the Roman occupation have always been a disputed topic. The Romans, by suppressing the war bands and plunderings of Belgic times,

---

[4] See Chapter Two.

brought a long, if somewhat interrupted, period of internal peace and security which allowed the development of a higher form of culture based on the civilization of the Mediterranean area—although, as we have seen, this development was attained at the cost of some economic depression for the native peasant population. Long-term influence on Britain's development is, however, a very different matter. The Latin way of life never penetrated Britain as deeply as it did other western provinces of the empire—and even by contemporary imperial standards these were the backward, underdeveloped areas of the Roman world, much inferior in both economic life and culture to the more sophisticated and prosperous lands of the eastern Mediterranean and northern Africa.

From the Roman point of view, Britain, although an important sector of the imperial frontier, was only a remote, thinly populated outpost of the empire. Romano-British society was always, in the main, a Celtic society somewhat superficially romanized. Most of the original "Roman" settlers after the Claudian invasion had come not from Italy but from Gaul, itself an area somewhat provincial in its culture, and Britain's standards compared with those of Italy rather as those of eighteenth-century America compared with Europe. Probably less than a third of the population enjoyed the advantages of Latin culture, and even most of these lived in the south and southeast.

It is easy to overestimate the importance of the towns and the villas, for these differed almost in kind rather than in degree from the greater town-and-villa systems of the continental empire. Even London—the greatest of the towns, the headquarters of the government, the hub of the road system, and the principal port—covered only 330 acres north of the Thames and a very small unwalled area south of the river. Its population probably did not exceed 15,000; the great theater at Constantinople could hold five times that number. Apart from London, there were about twenty so-called large towns, each with about 5,000 inhabitants. These were originally planned and built by military engineers rather than civilian architects—and somewhat clumsily at that. At Leicester the engineers had contrived to lead the aqueduct to the wrong point within the town. At Silchester they so inaccurately aligned the street grid that the portico of the bathhouse projected two feet into one of the main streets and, as a result of this mistake, the portico had to be pulled down, its columns cut off, and the stumps buried in the road.

This somewhat thin provincial culture unfortunately suffered attack from those barbarian tribes which had had least contact with Rome and least appreciation of the values, both material and moral, of Roman civilization. In the circumstances, the repeated withdrawal of troops from about 380 and the emperors' complete neglect of Britain after 410 left a hiatus in government which the local inhabitants had not been sufficiently trained to fill—or lacked the will to do so. Elsewhere, more cultivated barbarians, like Theodoric the Ostrogoth in northern Italy, who liked to regard himself as a Roman official, continued the Roman administrative system in their own areas. Nothing of this kind happened in Britain. Its administration vanished before a succession of piecemeal barbarian attacks until not a shadow of it remained, as elsewhere, for the barbarian successor states to build on.

It was the same with the towns and the villas. Although many of the towns were never completely abandoned, many being natural sites for what little trade there was under any economic circumstances, their inhabitants had degenerated into petty traders squatting among the ruins. None survived in sufficient vigor for its institutions to influence the development of the town government when new communities grew up in later centuries. And although at Withrington in Gloucestershire it has been shown that the boundaries of a seventh-century Saxon monastic estate coincide with those of a Roman villa and their great sheep flocks may have had a continuous existence, there is no proof of any continuity in estate administration. Roman government, culture, and economic organization left, at the most, only the faintest scratches on the slate.

The main Roman legacies were indirect, and one of the most important was the road system. Roman roads were the first to cut through the dense forests on the heavy clay soils in the valley areas. They thus not only made easier the ultimate Saxon penetration of the country but remained fundamentally important until the railway network was constructed in the nineteenth century. Because these roads converged on London they were probably a prime factor of that city's ultimately becoming the country's capital. Although some were built for commercial purposes, the major Roman roads were, in the main, intended to serve military needs, while the minor, local roads, which were built during the period of medieval settlement, were in their day more vital to the needs of the inhabitants.

Of equal, if not greater, importance was the spiritual development which came with the Christian religion. Introduced into the island as early as the second century, Christianity may at first have been a faith confined to a small number of eastern traders. By 314 an episcopate based upon the towns existed, but, owing to Britain's insularity, what had become by that time the principal official cult of the empire was remarkably slow to spread. Pagans were still erecting temples as late as 360 to 380. By 380, however, Christianity was passing from the urban aristocracy to the villas, whence it rapidly spread to the general population. Before the turn of the century, it had become the leading spiritual influence in the country, and, together with a revival of Celtic influence in art, it formed the basis of a distinctive sub-Roman culture, particularly in the southwest and in Wales, areas which kept some contact with the Mediterranean world long after the eastern part of the island had been cut off from the Continent. Christians took the lead in the Celtic struggle for survival against the Anglo-Saxons, and later in the seventh century the Celtic church profoundly influenced the tone of Anglo-Saxon Christianity.

CHAPTER TWO

The Roman occupation of Britain had very little influence on the future development of English institutions, economic or political. In the final analysis, that occupation turned out to have been nothing more than a superficial, if prolonged, military settlement. Although it took the Anglo-Saxon tribal bands several generations to conquer the territory that the Roman legions had conquered in one, the effects of their slow and gradual penetration were much more enduring. The village settlements, agricultural patterns, and local government organization which slowly evolved between the barbarian invasions and the Norman Conquest of 1066 last, most of them, to the present day. There are few modern villages whose names are not found in the great Anglo-Norman survey of 1087, known as Domesday Book, and the counties, the local government areas of modern England, came into being at the same time.

The Anglo-Saxon Immigrations

The earliest Anglo-Saxon warriors did not enter the country as casual predatory raiders or land-hungry settlers. In the early fifth century the British looked upon the Picts as their main enemy. To meet this ancient,

The Development
of Anglo-Saxon England

but ever more menacing, threat, they employed bands of Saxon mercenaries to garrison especially vulnerable areas. The first of these bands are thought to have arrived, possibly from the lower Rhine area, about 430, at the invitation of a British "tyrant" Vortigern. In 442 they rebelled against their employers, and, although the British put up a good fight, the rebellion opened the way to their fellows from overseas.

The new invasions generally took place along the rivers and the river valleys. Angle and Saxon raiders penetrated through the Humber and the Wash, up the Trent and the Ouse to the Midlands; more Angles and Saxons entered along the Thames estuary, the banks of the Stour in the southeast, and the joint estuary of the Waveney and the Yare in East Anglia. With the exception of the Humber and the Thames, these rivers were small, but they were deep enough to take the raiders' shallow, undecked, twenty-eight oared boats far inland.

The British put up a very stubborn fight, so stubborn that some of the invaders gave up their attempts at settlement and returned to their own countries. This period of fierce resistance, which reached a climax about 500 with a great British victory at an unidentified site called Mons Badonicus, later came to be associated with the tradition of twelve great battles against the heathen and developed into one of the greatest

ANGLO-SAXON ENGLAND

Forests

0 20 40 60 80
SCALE IN MILES

Tay

LINDISFARNE

NORTHUMBRIA

NORTH SEA

Ruthwell

Bewcastle

Jarrow
Wearmouth
Durham

Whitby

Stamford
Bridge

Fulford

IRISH SEA

Ouse   *Humber*

Lincoln

Trent

*THE
WASH*

Wrexham

Nottingham

Burton

MERCIA
Tamworth

Stamford

THE FENS

Yare

Waveney

Leicester

Tettenhall

Huntingdon

Northampton

Cambridge

*ST. GEORGE'S
CHANNEL*

Bedford

Stour

Severn

ICKNEILD WAY

Hertford

Maldon

Lea

Dorchester-
on-Thames

Thames

London

*ISLE OF
THANET*

Chepstow

Malmesbury

Rochester

Chippenham

Canterbury

Medway

Ellendune

Dover

Wedmore

WESSEX

KENT

Sedgemoor
Aethelney

Edington

SALISBURY PLAIN

Wilton

Winchester

Hastings

Sherborne

Pevensey

Tamar

ENGLISH CHANNEL

OFFA'S DYKE

WATLING STREET

Map of Anglo-Saxon England. (Adapted from F. M. Stenton, *Anglo-Saxon England*, Clarendon Press, Oxford.)

medieval romances—the Arthurian legend. For two generations and more, quiet and peace prevailed. Then about 550 the Anglo-Saxons successfully renewed their advance, but unlike the Romans they had no inherent military superiority over their opponents, so their conquest of the country took several generations. Campaigns and battles where the advantage fell now to one side, now to the other, coincided with a slow, more peaceful, and continuing process of immigration, whereby the land gradually passed into the hands of new owners. The final conquest of much of midland and southeastern England (the lowland zone) took place between 550 and 600; that of the north perhaps slightly later.

Warfare and Warlords

Anglo-Saxon England was born of warfare, remained forever a military society, and came to its end in battle. War always absorbed much of its energies: war against the Welsh; war among its own small, conflicting kingdoms; and war against external invaders. The scale of medieval warfare was minute: armies rarely exceeded a few thousand men.[1] Even so, this minute scale was enough to dominate the tone and customs of society, breeding a people accustomed to violence, with highly developed predatory instincts. The vital bond of society was the war band, or *comitatus*, of the lord and his followers, given over to the fighting quest for plunder and gold. Anglo-Saxon poets always gave a foremost place to gold, gems, and plunder when they sang of their visions of the world—

> There once many a man
> Mood-clad, gold bright, of gleams garnished,
> Flushed with wine-pride, flashing war-gear,
> Gazed on wrought gem-stones, on gold, on silver,
> On wealth held and hoarded, on light-filled amber.

—the aristocratic ideal of an heroic society where the greatest accumulations of wealth came from successful violence, or, to put it another way, where theft and superficial, barbaric splendor glittered against the drab, harsh poverty of a low-level agrarian economy.

The desirable attributes of the warlords who led these bands, and later of the kings who succeeded them, were great physical strength, a fine

---

[1] In 1066 William the Norman conquered England with as few as 5,000 Frenchmen, and toward the end of the thirteenth century Edward I waged his greatest campaigns with no more than 10,000 cavalry and 2,000 infantry.

presence, and a passionate temperament, expressing itself through ruth-
lessness, bravery, and lavish generosity. Even the supposedly saintly
Edward the Confessor was a far from gentle creature. His earliest biographer, who wrote only a few months after his death, described him as
"a very proper figure of a man, of outstanding height," "a man of passionate temper and of prompt and vigorous action" who could be as
terrible as a lion when anything roused his temper.[2] In the late eleventh
century, in Anglo-Norman times, Stephen, Count of Blois, praised his
father-in-law, William the Conqueror, as a man who "gave many and
great gifts."[3]

Generosity and shares in loot bound fighters to their chieftains: one
of the ever-recurring themes in epic poetry was the appeal to the memory
of great benefits received, of feasting, drinking, and bragging on past
exploits in the chieftain's hall. As the poem about the battle of Maldon in
991 put it, "Remember now our speeches that we spoke at the drinking of
mead, when we sat boasting, heroes in hall, of the stress of conflict; and
now it is come to the proof."[4] The proof, the return for the lord's distribution of rewards and wealth, was to follow him to the last, to death if need
be. Thus Wiglaf in the epic *Beowulf* rebuked his companions when they
refused to follow the king in his last, desperate enterprise: "I remember
how we promised our lord at the feast in hall when he gave us rings,[5] that
we would make him requital for the armour he gave us, rings and good
swords, if need should befall, as it now has befallen."

This vigorous, barbaric attitude was all pervasive. It penetrated even
Christianity. The Anglo-Saxon Christ was very much the contemporary
heroic warrior. The poem "A Dream of the Rood" describes his crucifixion:
"Then the young hero who was God Almighty, stripped himself strong and
steadfast. Bold in the sight of many he mounted the high cross where he
must redeem mankind. I trembled when he touched me, but I durst not bow
to the ground."

There was nothing in this society of the idea of the state as known
in the ancient world. The personal bond between man and man, based on
military prowess and the hope of profit, became the main bond of society.
As King Edward the Elder (899–925) exhorted his men at Exeter, "They
should all search out how their peace might be better than it had been. He
asked who would apply himself to its amendment, and be in that fellowship
that he was, and love that which he loved, and shun that which he
shunned."[6]

[2] *The Life of King Edward the Confessor*, ed. and trans. by F. Barlow (London, 1962),
p. 12.
[3] Quoted from R. H. C. Davis, *King Stephen, 1135-1154* (London, 1967), p. 2.
[4] K. Grossley-Holland and B. Mitchell, *The Battle of Maldon and Other Old English
Poems* (London, 1965), pp. 29 ff.
[5] Probably coats of mail made of iron rings.
[6] Laws of Edward, in W. Stubbs, *Select Charters* (9th ed.; Oxford, 1921), p. 73.

Although the violence of society gradually diminished throughout the Middle Ages and later, the state alone never became strong enough to enforce law and order; lordship in various mutations—feudalism, bastard feudalism, clientage, personal relationships between the rich and the poor, the powerful and the weak—remained the fundamental bond of discipline. When the state remained weak and lacking in resources, as it did for many centuries, there was no feasible alternative to this type of government by the rich, by the local magnate of the countryside.

As they overran England the war leaders assigned lands to their followers and ruled over them, but for a long time no single kingdom was established over the whole country. During the sixth century petty kings and kingdoms fought bitterly against each other and against the Welsh and the British in the west and southwest. The details of this period are clouded in obscurity. It is not until the seventh century, when England was converted to Christianity and we have the writings of the missionaries and the great Northumbrian historian Bede (c. 673–735), that there is sure evidence of contemporary events.

Certain kings began to establish powerful, if rather ill-defined, over-lordships over the others. By the eighth century these leaders were called "Bretwealdas"—the English version of the Latin *Rex Britanniae*, King of Britain.[7] From the beginning of the seventh century, three kingdoms became dominant in succession: Northumbria, Mercia, and Wessex.

The Northumbrian Kingdom

The first of the Bretwealdas was Edwin of Northumbria, who became a Christian in 627. Northumbria's military ascendancy may have derived from the inheritance of Romano-British buffer states. Its political pre-dominance continued to about 657, and until about eighty years later its culture was the most brilliant in Europe.

The origins of Northumbrian culture were extremely diverse. Some of its art motifs, introduced by Irish missionaries, are Celtic: the naturalistic motifs of animals and birds and the complicated arabesques so prominent in the decoration of the Lindisfarne Gospels. Other motifs are definitely Byzantine in origin. Since the barbarian invasions of Europe in the fifth century, the Byzantine provinces of Africa and the East had been far more cultivated than those of the West. When the Arabs invaded the provinces of North Africa and Asia Minor, their Greek-speaking inhabitants fled in increasing numbers to Europe. There was even a Greek cultural revival in

[7] The Bretwealdas were Aelle of the West Saxons (c. 477–91), Caelwin of the West Saxons (c. 560–84), Aethelbert of Kent (584–616), Raedwald of East Anglia (600–16), Edwin of Northumbria (616–32), Oswald of Northumbria (633–41), Oswiu of Northumbria (641–70).

Gold and niello buckle from Sutton Hoo burial mound, *c.* A.D. 655. (Courtesy of the British Museum.)

Rome from about 650 to 750, with a Greek colony around the church of Santa Maria in Cosmedin, and from 685 to 752 most of the Popes were of Eastern origin, either Greeks or Syrians. In the north, however, Byzantine influence was indirect, inspired by ivory miniatures and textiles imported from the eastern Mediterranean. Deriving from these, Northumbrian stone crosses, like those at Ruthwell and Bewcastle, show the development of a new school of sculpture and decoration, purely oriental in its inspiration based upon Syrian motifs of a vine-scroll interwoven with figures of birds and beasts.

Benedict Biscop (d. 690), the founder of the twin monasteries Wearmouth–Jarrow, intensely admired all things Roman, and during six visits to Rome he studied the life and customs of the Roman Church so that he could introduce them to his countrymen at home. He brought back with him foreign workmen to build churches, fabrics, and precious metals to decorate those churches and books for his monastery. He adopted from Canterbury Roman methods of education which Theodore of Tarsus, the papal nominee to the archbishopric, and his companion, Abbot Hadrian, has recently introduced there. At the same time, in spite of their Latin training, Benedict's monks still cherished the strange, unearthly poetry of the Germanic invaders, with its heroes and monsters, its grim humor, and its cryptic dialogue.

Although this culture attained its fullest and most complete expression in Northumbria, it reached a high level in other parts of the country as well. If late seventh- and early eighth-century Northumbria could claim the Venerable Bede, Wessex could boast of Aldhelm (*c.* 640–709), Abbot of Malmesbury and Bishop of Sherbourne, the first Englishman known to have written Latin verse. There are few material remains of Northumbrian civilization: a few churches or parts of churches which escaped later rebuilding in new styles; fragments of a wooden coffin, that of St. Cuthbert, at Durham; a few stone crosses; and illuminated books of marvelous quality, of which the finest and most famous is the Lindisfarne Gospels.

Bede, to whom ninth-century Franks gave the title "Venerable," may be called the first articulate Englishman. According to his own account, from the age of seven he lived within the walls of Wearmouth–Jarrow observing monastic discipline "and the daily care of singing in the church, and always took delight in learning, teaching and writing."[8] Although his life was circumscribed, his learning was far-ranging. For Bede himself, his theological works were all important; he would have been surprised to know that his enduring fame was to rest on his *Ecclesiastical History of the English People.*

Bede's *Ecclesiastical History* remains our finest account of early England. His achievement was remarkable, in that he was a pioneer historian with no models to guide him. Except for his treatment of Mercia, he was comparatively impartial. Bede's remarkable critical power knew no parallel

---

[8] *Bede's Ecclesiastical History of the English Nation*, Everyman Edition (London, 1910, 1951), p. 283.

Northumbrian art: The Franks Casket, *c.* A.D. 700. (Courtesy of the British Museum.)

St. Matthew from the Lindisfarne Gospels, c. A.D. 700. (Courtesy of the British Museum.)

in his own day; he never attempted to pad his works with romantic inventions. He distinguished carefully among types of sources—tradition, rumor, eye-witness accounts—and he often quoted entire documents which he obtained from as far afield as Canterbury and Rome. Above all, his style was lucid, clear, and flexible, quite unlike the grandiloquent pomposity favored by so many Latin authors of the Dark Ages. Bede may also have invented our method of reckoning time from the Christian era, although some historians now claim this distinction for a group of Frankish monks a century earlier.

The Golden Age of Northumbrian culture lasted from the Debate of Whitby (664)[9] to the death of Bede (735), but its influence in Europe, already pronounced, reached its height somewhat later in the eighth century. Never before or since has England occupied so unique a position in European civilization as during this Northumbrian efflorescence of art and letters. In the eighth century even Rome itself sought manuscripts from England. Anglo-Saxon missionaries converted the heathen east of the Rhine. Calling themselves the *milites Christi*, or "soldiers of Christ," courageous pioneers and adventurers still in the warrior tradition, they followed their religious lord with the same spirit and enterprise with which their fore-

[9] See below, p. 37.

bears had followed their pagan leaders. St. Boniface, the most renowned of them all, almost demanded martyrdom when, before an assembly of heathens, he cut down the sacred Oak of Thunor at Geismar in Prussia. Their admiration of his courage, in fact, saved his life for many more years of heroic missionary enterprise. Beside his work in what is now Germany, at the invitation of Pepin, Charlemagne, and his brother Carloman, Boniface began to reform the decadent Frankish church, bringing it into a closer relationship with Rome and thus increasing the power of the papacy. Later, the next generation of scholars, led by Alcuin of York, a pupil of one of Bede's disciples, carried Northumbrian educational methods to Aachen and Tours in France, where they contributed to the famous revival of Carolingian art and letters.

Northumbria at most, however, exercised a somewhat vague political hegemony. Geographically, it was too unfavorably placed and, in the early eighth century, became too unstable internally to unite the whole country. The idea of the country as a single political unit had survived from Roman times, but now it was the Roman priest rather than the Roman soldier who took the first step toward it. Unity came first to the Church and then, by example, to the state. Though both Roman and Celtic missionaries had converted different parts of England to Christianity, a period of bitter division and rivalry between the two churches delayed their unification. These differences were, to some extent, settled at the Debate of Whitby in 664. This settlement made possible the ultimate unity of the Anglo-Saxon Church and left the way open to superior Roman discipline and organization.

The next development came, as it were, almost by accident. Wighard, the Archbishop-elect of Canterbury, died in Rome in 667, and the Pope named Theodore of Tarsus to the vacancy. Theodore was then sixty-six, an enormous age for that period. Educated in the still cultivated and civilized Byzantine empire, he had a great reputation as a scholar and a philosopher. What he thought of the prospect of ending his days in the cold, barbaric north nobody knows, but even in old age he displayed immense vigor, drive, and organizing ability. As well as revising the discipline of the English Church, his work led to extremely important political results. Starting with the Synod of Hertford in 672, he summoned a series of councils which brought together the bishops and the more important ecclesiastics of the entire country. At Hertford the archbishop planned annual synods to take place each August at Cloveshoh.[10] These synods, or general councils, promulgated canons valid for the Church as a whole, thus ignoring the boundaries of the provincial kingdom, so that the Church first set the example of legislation valid for the whole land. It is, of course, easy to exaggerate the Church's influence upon a people still, and for long after, only superficially Christianized. Most of the priesthood was ill-educated and unable to explain adequately the dogmas upon which the Church's ritual and liturgy were based, so that a parallel belief in pagan practices

---

[10] This place has never been identified.

remained and, in many areas, took centuries to die away. In organization, however, Theodore's synods marked a step forward in the breakdown of provincial separatism. The Church served as a powerful example. Yet it could not, of itself, bring about political unity. In the final analysis, unity, under the kingdom of Wessex, was the product of the sword: "War makes the king!"

The Mercian Kingdom

Meanwhile, Northumbrian ascendancy gave way to that of Mercia, and the remnants of Northumbrian culture perished in the ninth-century Viking raids. Owing to lack of evidence, historians have only recently recognized the achievements of the Mercian kingdom. Bede, who so much admired the Christian civilization of Northumbria, found it difficult to concede that anything good could come out of a pagan state such as Mercia had been until the middle of the seventh century. However, Bede completed his *Ecclesiastical History* in 731, before the greatest days of Mercian supremacy under King Offa (758–96). The Mercians themselves produced no chronicles, or at least none that have survived. The Danish occupation of the ninth and tenth centuries wiped out the historical landmarks and traditions of this midland kingdom, and the chronicles of the West Saxon house, the dynasty which ultimately united the country, were not inclined to praise a kingdom which their countrymen had so often fought. Yet even King Alfred spoke with respect of the code of laws (now lost) which Offa issued. It is true that Mercian civilization was not as brilliant as that of Northumbria; it was of a different type, but it should not be underestimated.

From their original settlements near the middle of the River Trent, the Mercians had pushed their way gradually towards the borders of Wales. As G. O. Sayles has written, "These hardy folks had undertaken a task from which the Britons had always flinched: they had with undaunted courage waged a long and relentless war upon nature, overcoming their superstitious terrors to overthrow the impenetrable forests and drain the marshes and cut down the reed-beds. The military victories of their neighbours pale into insignificance besides this economic triumph."[11] It has also been suggested that Mercia's supremacy was based, at least in part, on commerce, although, on the contrary, this commerce may possibly have been the result of its eventual dominance over England rather than the basis upon which that dominance was built. Whatever the truth may be, Mercia certainly had strong international connections. It exported woolen cloth and cloaks to the territories of Emperor Charlemagne, and the trade was extensive enough for the length of the cloths exported to be standard-

[11] G. O. Sayles, *The Medieval Foundation of England*, 2nd ed. (London, 1950), p. 65.

ized in a commercial agreement of 796. Mercia's economic connections have been shown by the discovery of its coins overseas. One of Offa's gold coins found near Rome is an imitation of a Moslem coin, the dinar, issued by the caliph in 774. Moreover, Offa, in the later part of his reign, issued new and heavier silver coins, commonly known as pennies, and it is most likely that from this time 240 pennies came to represent a pound. This relationship is exactly that which prevailed under Charlemagne from about 780, at the latest, and remained a standard monetary relationship for centuries. This conformity must be the sign of a close connection between English and Frankish trade at this time. Offa's position must have been powerful internationally, for after Charlemagne's defeat of the Avars the emperor sent him cloaks, an Avar sword, and a sword belt.

Mercia's achievements at home indicate that it possessed what was for the times a powerful organization. Its most impressive monument is Offa's Dyke, a great ditch and earthwork running from the Irish Sea to the Bristol Channel, from the neighborhood of Wrexham to that of Chepstow, as a defense against the Welsh. It has been called the greatest public work of the Anglo-Saxon period, and its scale implies a long period of internal peace and very considerable resources.

Nor were Mercia's administrative achievements in their way less impressive. There exists a document (or part of one) known as the Tribal Hidage, which most authorities now agree comes from the days of Mercian ascendancy. It lists a number of districts, or regions, enumerating the households of families which they contained; regions covering a large territory in the Midlands, Kent, Sussex, East Anglia, Essex, and Wessex. Such marshalin;, of information shows that the Mercian monarchy could, by contemporary standards, deploy considerable administrative powers. Moreover, a comparison of Mercian charters with those of lesser kingdoms shows them to be much more developed and seems to indicate a real distinction between primitive government in the local kingdoms and the beginning of a real administrative routine at the Mercian court.

The Mercian kings evolved a political system which included every kingdom in southern England. It was not uniform. At some points, it probably meant little more than occasional hospitality shown to the Mercian kings by local rulers. But, at the other end of the scale, more than one insignificant local king exchanged independence for the more secure position of a provincial "ealdorman"[12] under Mercia. In particular, by showing that the particularism of local kings could be overcome, the system marked a distinct advance toward the political unity of England.

In the last analysis, the reasons for Mercia's failure to survive are uncertain. Its supremacy was, perhaps, premature: other kingdoms, Wessex

---

[12] An official ruling on behalf of the king. After the Danish invasion, the term was replaced by the Scandinavian title "earl."

and East Anglia, were still too strong, and because its domination of the lesser kingdoms relied entirely upon military force, it never inspired a countrywide sentiment of loyalty. The Mercian system was also largely a personal creation, dependent upon the strong personalities of its kings, and after Ceolwulf I (831–33) these rulers seem to have been lesser men. Nor were they of the old royal blood, and the petty provincial kings probably felt less respect for them.

Wessex: King Alfred and the Danish Invasions

It was the third great English state, Wessex, that gave the country the last of its Bretwealdas, or overlords, and the first of its territorial kings ruling without royal rivals. The supremacy of the royal house of Wessex also came from its prowess in war, but war of a new kind which encouraged a loyal sentiment to gather about its leaders: war this time not against a brother kingdom, but war against violent, ruthlessly destructive foreign invaders.

The problem of the origins of the West Saxons is even more obscure than many other intractable problems of this obscure age. Judging from archaeological evidence, the main body of West Saxons, coming via the Fens and the Ickneild Way or along the Thames, arrived about the year 500 near Dorchester-on-Thames, where they settled in considerable numbers. The Anglo-Saxon *Chronicle*, the chief literary source of the period, however, is completely silent about this migration. It claims that the West Saxons originally arrived on the south coast, entered the country through Southampton Water and Hampshire, reaching Dorchester about 550. A plausible theory suggests that both migrations took place, but the chronicler, interested in the dynasty and not the people, relates only the movements of the southern group, which fostered the royal family.

Pressure from Mercia drove the West Saxons to abandon their original settlements around Dorchester and to move west. Under King Ine (688–726) they occupied Somerset, Dorset, and Devon. Under his leadership they also began to expand eastward, imposing a temporary control over the kings of Kent, Sussex, and Surrey. By 779, however, Offa of Mercia had imposed his overlordship on Wessex, and it was not until 802 when Egbert (802–39), the West Saxon claimant, returned from exile that Wessex made any further progress. In 825 Egbert defeated the Mercians at Ellendune. Although recognized then as Bretwealda, his effective supremacy over the Midlands was short-lived. He did, however, once and for all unite England south of the Thames.

The disaster which now swept over the West Saxon monarchy was not the result of internal disturbances and the rise of rival kingdoms, like the end of the Northumbrian and Mercian supremacies. The country's wealth once again attracted the greed of foreign invaders. The wandering of peoples which had brought the Anglo-Saxons to England had not yet ceased. Now, in the late eighth century, driven partly by overpopulation, partly by distaste for the more authoritarian government then being imposed on Denmark, the Scandinavians swept out of the Baltic north in predatory waves which took them as far afield as Moscow and Kiev, Greenland and the Mediterranean, a vigorous barbarian onslaught which almost overwhelmed the precariously balanced civilization of western Europe.

Until 850 these Scandinavian raids on England, though increasingly frequent, were mostly predatory. But then, instead of returning home after the season's raids, they, for the first time, wintered in the Isle of Thanet off the coast of Kent. With the appearance of the Danish "Great Army" in 865, a concerted plan of conquest seems to become apparent. During the next few years, the Danes destroyed Northumbria and established kingdoms of their own in York and East Anglia. They followed these triumphs by overrunning parts of Mercia and Wessex. In Wessex King Aethelraed and his brother Alfred, who succeeded him in 871, fought a series of obstinate but inconclusive battles, and in 872 Alfred was obliged to bribe off his foes. From then on Alfred's whole life was a prolonged series of struggles. Before his death in 899, he was forced to wage three major wars against the Danes. During the intervals of peace he was responsible for initiating a major reorganization of government. In 878 the Danes occupied Chippenham. It seemed as though the last independent English kingdom was about to fall. But Alfred, from the remote royal estate at Aethelney on Sedgmoor in the marshy lands of Somerset, harried the Danes throughout the spring, and rallying the forces of the shires of Somerset, Wiltshire, and Hampshire, he defeated them at Edington, on the northern slopes of Salisbury Plain. The Danish leader Guthrum accepted baptism, abandoned the attempt to subject Wessex, and retired to establish a Danish colony in East Anglia.

Edington marked the turning point in Alfred's career, but his battles were by no means over. He was forced to defend the Thames estuary both by land and by sea against Danish attacks. In 884 a new army landed in Kent (one that had already raided there six years earlier), assisted by the Danes of East Anglia. This assistance, by people already firmly based in England, made the attacks really dangerous. Alfred, therefore, sent a punitive expedition to East Anglian waters: it captured sixteen ships at the mouth of the River Stour, but it was defeated before it returned to harbor.

In 886 the West Saxons occupied London, which had been in Danish hands since 872. The acquisition of London was of the greatest strategical and political importance, for it marked out Alfred as the leader of the whole English people. As the Anglo-Saxon *Chronicle* said, "All the English people who were not under the Danes submitted to Alfred." Alfred and Guthrum now made the Treaty of Wedmore, which made Watling Street, the

Ouse, the Lea, and the Thames the frontier line between the peoples under English and those under Danish rule and law.

Alfred had to fight yet a third war to beat off a new Danish invasion in 893, and sporadic warfare continued for the next four years. This time he was less successful, although there was never any serious danger of the English resistance collapsing as completely as it had collapsed in the early seventies. Throughout this last war, the initiative remained always with the Danes, for they had the advantage of a secure base in the territories won by their predecessors in the north and east. The main Danish army dispersed in the summer of 896. Some joined the allies in East Anglia and Northumbria, while others, who had made nothing from the war, apparently threw in their lot with another Danish army attacking France through the Seine. Even so, raids on Britain were not yet over. Until 910 armies from one or another of the Danish colonies continued to invade Wessex territory.

The inconclusiveness of these later years did not destroy what King Alfred had already achieved, and his reorganization of the military system made possible a territorial advance under his successors. The defense of Wessex lay almost completely upon the peasant levies of the shires, a non-professional force drawn from the farming population of the countryside. Defense at this time was always far more difficult to organize than aggressive raids. With the incentive of plunder lacking, and consumed by anxiety about the harvests upon which its very existence for the coming year depended, the peasant militia was often most unwilling to serve outside its own districts, and the militiamen often dispersed before the season's campaign was over. No king at this time was ever strong enough to force men to stay under arms against their will. Alfred, therefore, had to attack the problem indirectly. The method which he adopted was to divide the shire militias into two parts: one half stayed at home on their farms to look to their vital crops while the other section was out in the field against the Danes. Thus, the peasant levies could be kept in action longer than ever before. One of the most striking features of Alfred's last war was the much greater mobility and wider range of his troops. He also stiffened these peasant levies by a more professional group, a force of mounted infantry made up of household retainers of the king and of the greater "thegns"[13] of the shires.

The invaders came from the sea, and communication at sea was always a most important factor in determining the course of war. The Danes of Northumbria and East Anglia were such a threat to the West Saxon kings because their sea power was a most effective support to newcomers from Scandinavia. Alfred was probably never without ships. In 884 he had been able to send a fleet into East Anglian waters, but the Danes probably

---

[13] Men who owned at least five hides of land—that is, the more prominent landowners. See also p. 59.

possessed larger craft than any available to the king. Alfred, therefore, embarked upon a naval program and by 897 had constructed a fleet of ships said to have been larger and faster than any foreign vessels. According to the Anglo-Saxon *Chronicle*, the king himself designed them—but these ships were not entirely successful, for the Frisian sailors hired to man them found them difficult to operate.

The defense of southern England had also been hampered by the absence or rarity of fortifications. Alfred commanded the construction of a series of fortresses, or "burhs." We gain most of our information about these structures from a document called the Burghal Hidage, compiled during the reign of Alfred's son Edward (899–925)—but there is reason to believe that Alfred laid down the main outline of this defensive system before the Danish invasion of 892. By the early part of the tenth century, no district in Sussex, Surrey, or Wessex east of the River Tamar was more than twenty miles from a fortress. The inhabitants of the surrounding countryside had to bear the cost of building, maintaining, and garrisoning the fortresses, and, according to Asser, Alfred's biographer, who lived for several years at the royal court, this burden was unpopular—a statement which seems to be borne out by the fact that the only resistance which confronted the invaders of 892 on their landing came from a few peasants sitting in a half-made fort.

A generation of looting, rapine, and devastation left King Alfred the task of reviving a war-stricken, impoverished, and demoralized society. Alfred himself may have exaggerated the effects of the wars, but there is no doubt that reconstruction was essential. Successful war leaders have not always proved themselves brilliant in civilian affairs, but King Alfred was a notable exception, both in legislation and in the revival of education which made further social progress possible.

Alfred issued a collection of laws, drawing upon all that was best in the earlier codes of Aethelbert, Ine, and Offa. To tighten the bonds of social discipline, several clauses in particular stressed one of the strongest, most recent trends in society: the growth of lordship, that is, the imposition of public order and control through great and powerful local men that has already been described.[14] Every man was to place himself in the jurisdiction of a lord. In the future, death was the penalty for disloyalty to a lord or to the king, and a man might fight for his lord without becoming liable to a vendetta.

Alfred, like another great warlord, the Emperor Charlemagne—Charles the Great of the Franks—a century earlier, had a high ideal of kingship, seeing it as a divine Christian trust for the benefit of the people. Like Charlemagne, he advocated a practical, Christian education as a remedy for the current evils of society. Like Charlemagne, he developed a "Palace

[14] See above, pp. 32–33 and below, pp. 48, 58–59.

School," to which he brought scholars from more cultivated areas outside the realm. Alfred's school, however, was a school with a difference: it was a center of vernacular as well as of Latin culture, and unlike Charlemagne, who was illiterate, Alfred himself became its most notable author. Although Alfred said (probably with some exaggeration) that knowledge of Latin had almost disappeared, he did not, as is sometimes stated, look upon Anglo-Saxon as a mere second-best language. He regarded the two languages in different ways: Latin as essential for advanced education and culture; Anglo-Saxon for government. Alfred himself learned enough Latin to translate Pope Gregory the Great's *Pastoral Care* and the *World History of Orosius*, as well as commissioning other translations. Except for the *Consolation of Philosophy* of Boethius, he chose his books for their practical utility, almost as textbooks for training in ecclesiastical and public life. According to Asser, he told his followers, "I wonder at your assurance that, having taken upon yourselves, by God's favour and mine, the rank and office of wise men, you have neglected the studies of the wise. Either abandon at once the exercise of the temporal powers that you possess, or endeavour more zealously to study the lessons of wisdom."[15]

In modern eyes, Alfred's educational program seems limited, dull, and prosaic indeed, but after all, it was well suited to the times, to the needs of a society sunk in illiteracy and ignorance. What became of his program in the end we do not know. The "Palace School" itself seems to have been short-lived, and none of Alfred's successors tried to develop this aspect of his work. In spite of Asser's somewhat improbable assurance that "wonderful to relate almost all his ealdormen and officials, though unlearned from childhood, gave themselves up to the study of letters, preferring an unfamiliar discipline to the loss of office,"[16] the warlike habits of the aristocracy and the condition of contemporary society were too adverse for the extensive development of lay education. Yet, in spite of this, Alfred's efforts produced a vernacular literature which had no counterpart in the contemporary world.

Alfred's descendants carried on the work of reconquest, and their military exploits deserve attention because of their contribution to the development of political unity. Although Alfred's defensive measures had made the possibility of a Danish conquest of the whole country remote, the future was still uncertain. However, his descendants were so successful that the Anglo-Saxon *Chronicle* remarked of his great-grandson, Edgar the Peaceable (959–75): "Kings remote, greatly honoured to the King submitted, was no fleet so insolent, no host so strong that in the Angle race took from him aught the while the noble King ruled in the royal seat." A reliable tradition tells that in 973 Edgar acted as steersman to a boat on the

---

[15] *Asser's Life of King Alfred*, ed. by W. H. Stevenson (Oxford, Eng., 1904, repr., 1959), Ch. 106.
[16] *Ibid.*

River Dee rowed by eight kings—Scottish, North British, Welsh, and Norse—thus showing in a symbolic way his superiority and lordship over them all.

After Alfred's death there was little action until the Danes, defeated in a campaign in 909, were compelled to make peace on terms dictated by Edward the Elder (899–925). When the Danes revolted against these terms the following year, Edward decisively defeated them at Tettenhall in Staffordshire—a defeat which left open the way for a great expansion of the West Saxon kingdom.

Nor were the Mercians idle. The year after Tettenhall, when Aethelraed of Mercia died, the Mercians accepted as their ruler his widow, Alfred's daughter and Edward the Elder's sister, Aethelflaeda, who ruled for the next eight years with the somewhat anomalous title of Lady of the Mercians. To have been accepted as the ruler of a warlike society, Aethelflaeda must have been a woman of quite extraordinary personality and ability, for she kept the loyalty of a formidable military household, personally led military expeditions, and, with a superb eye for country and for predicting the movements of the Danish army, built a series of burhs. She carried out year after year a deliberate plan of fortress building, which gave a new solidity to Mercia's defenses and by 917 enabled her to make her power felt in the lands both to the east and west of her own territories.

Aethelflaeda's brilliant organization in Mercia made possible her brother Edward's aggressive moves against the Danes, until by 918 only four Danish armies remained south of the Humber, grouped around Leicester, Stamford, Nottingham, and Lincoln. With their defeat, the frontier was carried north to the river. Then in 937 after another victory at Brunanburh (a site which has never been satisfactorily identified), Edward's son Aethelstan (925–40) was accepted as ruler from the English Channel to the Firth of Forth, though only as overlord in the far north.

These remarkable successes were due to three things: the family relationship of Edward and Aethelflaeda, the willingness of the Mercians to cooperate in times of danger, and the disunity of the Danes. The Wessex royal family was always careful of Mercian susceptibilities, but even so the cooperation was extraordinary, and not without its difficulties, for in 924 the men of Western Mercia were prepared to ally themselves with the Welsh against Edward. As for the Danes, at least five armies had taken part in the events of 917–18; but their efforts had been none too well coordinated, and, as time went on, this lack of unity became ever more pronounced.

In the last quarter of the century new and terrible disasters shattered this record of success. When Edgar the Peaceable died in 975, only two years after the brilliant ceremony on the Dee, troubles began almost at once. Edgar's widow murdered her stepson to win the throne for his younger half-brother Aethelraed (979–1016). Aethelraed was barely fourteen, and the rule of a minor always spelled trouble in medieval conditions. As the Bible puts it, "Woe unto the land when the King is a child." Nor were affairs much better when Aethelraed, commonly known as "the Redeless," or without counsel, attained his majority. At this time, according to the Anglo-Saxon *Chronicle,* "God's adversaries God's law broke, and ever afterwards it greatly grew in evil." Even allowing for the fact that the writer of this section of the *Chronicle* was violently prejudiced against Aethelraed, or at least against his advisers, it is a terrible record. Forces from Denmark and other parts of Scandinavia (the *Chronicle* briefly refers to them as "the Army") campaigned every year. Their devastations were appalling, and the defense of the country a pitiful, shameful story of unreadiness, treachery, shilly-shallying, and incompetence, until, at last, it broke down almost completely. Year after year the *Chronicle* records the Danish devastations, and it often records nothing else. It is worth quoting an entry in full, that for the year 999:

> This year came the army about again into the Thames, and went up thence along the Medway to Rochester; where the Kentish army came against them, and encountered them in a close engagement; but alas! they too soon yielded and fled; because they had not the aid they should have had. The Danes therefore occupied the field of battle, and, taking horse, they rode as wide as they would, spoiling and over-running nearly all West-Kent. Then the King with his council determined to proceed against them with sea and land forces; but as soon as the ships were ready, then arose delay from day to day, which harassed the miserable crew that lay on board; so that, always, the forwarder it should have been, the later it was, from one time to another; they still suffered the army of their enemies to increase; the Danes continually retreated from the sea-coast; and they continually pursued them in vain. Thus in the end these expeditions both by sea and land served no other purpose but to vex the people, to waste their treasure, and to strengthen their enemies.

The *Chronicle,* however, was unfair in its entirely one-sided allocation of blame. Disorganization there certainly was, but the collapse was to a great extent due to the appearance of a new and more professional type of Scandinavian army. The Danish forces of the ninth century had achieved their success because they had undisputed command of the sea, and they moved rapidly about the country on horses which they seized immediately, on their surprise landings, from the local population. In open battle, however, they had shown no marked superiority over the Anglo-Saxon levies. The Danes had come to colonize, and their victory was a means to that end. But by the late tenth century Scandinavian armies of a different type had come into being, armies which historians call the "Jomsburg type," after a fortress near the mouth of the River Oder, armies trained in a kind of primitive military academy there; highly trained professional soldiers whose purpose was not to colonize but to spend their lives fighting and plundering. Organized in tightly disciplined communities, the soldiers lived by raiding and levying tribute, which they carried back to their fortresses in Denmark.

At last, leading such a trained army, King Swein of Denmark attacked England, but, unlike the ninth-century raiders, he had the resources of a united kingdom behind him. Aethelraed fled the country, and from 1013 to 1042 Danish kings—Swein, his son Cnut, and Cnut's sons Harold and Harthacanut—ruled. Once the Danes had established themselves, the devastations ceased and Danish rule was far from being a curse. Although racial feeling existed, it was quite unlike modern nationalism; men were prepared to accept a foreign ruler who was capable of giving them internal peace and justice and who did not reward his alien followers too lavishly at their expense. After all, the West Saxon monarchs ruled a varied collection of English, Britons, Welsh, Norsemen, and Danes. There was no breach in either the continuity or the institutions of government: Cnut even married Aethelraed's widow Emma in the interests of political stability. Now there was peace, order, and good government such as the country had not known since the death of Edgar the Peaceable. Moreover, England became part of the great Scandinavian maritime empire, so English trade and towns probably drew considerable stimulus from this new Scandinavian connection.

Cnut's loosely connected empire (it was essentially a personal creation) quickly fell apart after his death in 1035, as his sons were unable to maintain his position. But it says a great deal for the now long-established tradition of political unity that the country did not divide on racial, Danish and Saxon, lines. Even those who had gained most from Danish rule joined in recalling from exile Aethelraed's only surviving son Edward, commonly known as "the Confessor," who reigned, in spite of chronic threats of invasion from Scandinavia, until his death in 1066.

CHAPTER THREE

The institutions of the Anglo-Saxon people hardly formed a constitution or a state, as we understand these terms today. Population was so thin, communication so slow and so poor, that distant provinces had to be left to the rule of local magnates, and even in areas closer to the royal court meager resources of necessity limited the activities of the central government. Kings were less concerned with the development of their own direct powers and jurisdiction than with seeing that other established authorities did their job efficiently. Then, and for a long time to come, the greater part of government was local government.

Law, Customs, the Shire, and the Hundred

Society was anchored in customary law. Kinship and lordship, rather than the coercive powers of central government, provided the bonds of social discipline. Today we think of law as originating with the central government, as a complicated, highly technical body of rules imposed and frequently and continuously altered for better or worse by legislation: a body of rules so abstruse that it needs a special profession for its interpretation

Anglo-Saxon
Institutions

and administration. This was not so before the twelfth century, at the earliest. The king did not dictate law. It lay theoretically changeless, timeless and immutable in the memory and custom of the people. Officials had nothing to do with its making, only with its enforcement. Each tribal region had its own peculiar law, and with new invasions complications increased as time went on. King Edgar the Peaceable (959–75), for example, conceded that the Danes of eastern England, in return for their loyalty, should live under such social and legal customs as they themselves might choose, apart from certain rules, particularly those for the suppression of cattle stealing, which should be universally observed. It is hardly surprising that within at most a generation of his reign the fifteen shires of the Danish area (a considerable part of the whole country) had come to be collectively known as the "Danelaw," a distinction which did not become obsolete until the time of Henry II (1154–89), when the circuits of his itinerant justices began to erode these local codes.

The law, then, was not an exterior authority: it was folk-right, and as such the people declared it in popular or folk courts, local assemblies of the people rather than government tribunals in the modern sense. In the late Anglo-Saxon period the two main courts were those of the shire and the hundred. Both were in full operation by the middle of the tenth century.

ANGLO-SAXON SHIRES IN THE EARLY ELEVENTH CENTURY

SCALE IN MILES

0 20 40 60 80

NORTH SEA

NORTHUMBERLAND

Carlisle
Durham

CUMBERLAND

ST. CUTHBERT'S LAND

Appleby

WESTMORLAND

UNSHIRED LANDS ANNEXED TO YORKSHIRE

IRISH SEA

Lancaster

YORK

York

BETWEEN RIBBLE AND MERSEY

Chester

DERBY

NOTTINGHAM

LINCOLN

Lincoln

CHESHIRE

STAFFORD

Derby

Nottingham

Stafford

NORFOLK

Shrewsbury

Tamworth

Norwich

ST. GEORGE'S CHANNEL

SHROPSHIRE

Leicester

LEICESTER

NORTHAMPTON

CAMBRIDGE

HUNTS.

WARWICK

Thatford

Warwick

Huntingdon

WORCESTER

Northampton

Cambridge

Bury St. Edmunds

HEREFORD

Worcester

Bedford

SUFFOLK

Ipswich

BEDS.

Hereford

Buckingham

Colchester

Hertford

Gloucester

OXFORD

BUCKS.

HERTFORD

ESSEX

GLOUCESTER

Oxford

MIDDLESEX

London

Cricklade

Wallingford

Reading

Rochester

WILTS.

BERKS.

Sandwich

Bristol

SURREY

Canterbury

SOMERSET

Salisbury

HANTS.

Guildford

KENT

Dover

Wilton

Winchester

Taunton

SUSSEX

DEVON

Southampton

Lewes

DORSET

Hastings

Launceston

Exeter

Dorchester

Wareham

CORNWALL

ENGLISH CHANNEL

Map of Anglo-Saxon shires in the early eleventh century. (Adapted from F. M. Stenton, *Anglo-Saxon England*, Clarendon Press, Oxford.)

The origins of the shire in different parts of the country were diverse. In the South it could represent an earlier kingdom which had been absorbed: Kent, Essex, and Sussex were shires of this kind. Other shires had been tribal divisions within a kingdom, like Norfolk and Suffolk which had made up the kingdom of East Anglia. Yet others were made up of the area around the nucleus of a large town: such were Dorset (Dorchester) and Wiltshire (Wilton). The first certain evidence for the existence of these southern shires dates from about 100 years before the reign of King Alfred. The Wessex kings created the shires as administrative units, accepting in some way or other traditional territorial divisions and creating other new ones. By Alfred's time, and in Alfred's laws, they can be seen fully at work as police, judicial, and military units. No man might leave his shire without permission. The shire moot or assembly sat in judgment on offenders. The ealdormen called out the armies on the basis of the shire.

This southern institution proved so useful that by the early part of the eleventh century the West Saxon kings had deliberately introduced it into the Midlands and the North. The older southern shires varied in size and were most irregular in shape. The new shires formed much neater arrangements. The chief towns—Leicester, Northampton, Huntingdon, Bedford, and Cambridge—were usually at their very center. Probably the Danish invasions, by destroying the traditional local divisions in the eastern half of the old Mercian kingdom, provided the opportunity for this new symmetrical rearrangement. Or it is possible that the shire represented an amount of land thought sufficient to provide enough men for the defense of the central burgh. This explanation will not, however, serve for Western Mercia where there was no Danish occupation. There the shire must have been a conscious, deliberate imitation of West Saxon methods of government.

From earliest times, however, smaller divisions than the shire must have existed. During the tenth century the district called "the hundred" came prominently into the plan of local government. Although it is impossible to be dogmatic about its origins or to connect it with earlier forms of local division, it provided the basis of public finance and justice. All that we can say is that the origins of the hundred are certainly diverse. Its size varied extremely in different parts of the country. It was as tiny as an eighth of a square mile or as large as eighteen square miles. Kent in the South had seventy-one such divisions, while, in the western Midlands and the North, Staffordshire and Lancashire had only five each. As in the shire, the tiny hundreds of the South probably represented older traditional areas, and the roughly symmetrical hundreds of the Midlands were again the result of a deliberate remodeling of administrative areas during the tenth century. One origin may lie in the royal vills or "tuns," whose bailiffs supervised the royal estates, collected levies and tolls, and punished criminals. The name of the unit and many of its functions may derive from what were originally voluntary associations for keeping the peace. It is said that voluntary peace-keeping associations, or frith-guilds, to carry out police duties, at first against cattle thieves, arranged for their guildsmen to be grouped in tens, or "tithings," to make up a hundred under a head man, called a "hundred man." The king was much concerned to use any means possible to improve standards of public order in a violent and disorderly society. Therefore, King Edgar, in his "Law of the Hundred," made the system compulsory for the whole country, probably associating the voluntary hundreds with the royal vills and giving them powers to try and punish offenders as well as to arrest them. By the time of Cnut's reign every free man was ordered to be in the supervision of the hundred.

The shire court met twice a year, the hundred every four weeks. As far as jurisdiction was concerned, the shire was in no way superior. It was not a court of appeal from the hundred. Both courts dealt with the same type of offenses, and most of the judicial business was transacted in the hundred—though the greatest cases, especially those which involved prominent men, tended to be heard in the shire, because, being a wider assembly, it gave greater publicity to its decisions.

Procedure in these courts was extremely primitive. At first, there was no conception of crime in the modern sense. Misdemeanors were offenses not against the state but against the group to which an injured person was bound by kinship or lordship. The main police problem, and a difficult one, was to produce the suspected party in one of the courts to answer for his offenses. Both this task and "police supervision" in general were carried out through a system of collective responsibility, that of the "bohr," or surety. This could be effected in three ways: by a man's kindred who were held responsible for his actions, by his lord, or by an artificial group. A lord could become a bohr for his servants and tenants, and such lordship was always of paramount importance. Parallel to this, in early days the kindred[1] were held responsible for the offenses of their members. Later, as the ties of kindred became less effective—or, at least, as people thought that possibly the kindred might give prejudiced and unfair protection to their erring members—society more and more stressed the authority of the lord and also moved to a collective security system based on the locality or territory. As previously implied, later Anglo-Saxon laws required every male over the greater part of the country, unless exempted by high social position or great wealth, to be enrolled for police purposes in a tithing, or a group of ten people. If a member of a tithing became involved in wrongdoing, his fellow members were obliged to produce him for trial or to pay a

---

[1] A kindred group probably extended to six degrees, that is, fourth cousins.

fine for dereliction of duty and compensation to the injured party. Thus, legally and socially, a man could hardly exist as an individual. Before the law he must find the protection and discipline of kindred, lord, or tithing. As King Aethelstan's (925–40) laws put it:

> And we have ordained respecting those lawless men of whom no law can be got that the kindred be commanded that they domicile him to folk-right, and find him a lord in the folk-moot; and if they will not or cannot produce him at the term, then he be henceforth a "flyma," and let him slay him for a thief who can come at him; and whoever after that shall harbour him, let him pay for him according to his "wer" or by it clear himself.

Group responsibility and group security were, then, the very essentials of existence: below a certain social level, the lone man, outside the group, could hardly be said to live.

Once kindred, lord, or tithing had hauled the offender into court[2] (often a far from easy task), he faced conditions and procedures quite different from those of today. Scientific methods for taking, examining, and sifting evidence lay a long way in the future. Impotent in their own limitations, men felt that the decision in any particular case lay in the will of God, who would make his pleasure manifest if the court followed certain traditional, well-defined procedures. The whole ethos of justice was highly mystical, and in the absence of modern methods of evidence and proof the courts laid great emphasis on elaborate procedures, formulae, and formalities. If these were correctly performed, then and only then would the divine intention be revealed. God's will could be ascertained in one of two ways: by oath or by ordeal. The obligatory personal oath of the accused repudiating his alleged offenses was not enough. He had to produce his kin or other sureties as compurgators, or oath-helpers, to support his oath and to declare it a true one. How many compurgators a man had to produce depended on a number of factors: his social position, the seriousness of his crime, and his own reputation, good or bad, among his neighbors. If he failed to find compurgators willing to support him or if he failed at the ordeal, thus manifesting guilt, he had to pay a "bot," or damages, to the injured party and a "wite," or fine, to the court.

Monarchy and the Law

It might well be thought that in this custom-bound, localized society there was very little scope for monarchy. Indeed, in remote Iceland, under isolated, peaceful conditions, a similar system worked quite well without it. In England, however, the need for defense—first of the local kingdoms

2 See p. 61.

against each other, later against the Danes—made vigorous leadership essential. Moreover, all societies develop, and their institutions come to need adjustment. Only the leadership of monarchy, by overcoming the inbuilt inertia of these custom-ridden communities, could introduce such necessary changes. Kings, above all, worked to improve standards of public order, and in their efforts to do so they stressed the welfare of the whole community, rather than the established individual rights with which the customary law was overwhelmingly concerned. To establish the interest of the entire community over that of the individual, kings used the process of legislation. Indeed, we have more new codes of law from Anglo-Saxon England than from any other country of Western Europe during these centuries—all, or most of them, issued to meet somewhat exceptional circumstances.

Although the folk normally looked on the law as immutable custom which it was their duty to preserve, difficulties arose from time to time. Certain passages of the law might become obscure, new circumstances might arise which the law did not cover, or the law might become difficult to enforce after periods of war and disorder. That passages of law might become obscure is easy enough to imagine. The second difficulty, that of new circumstances, seems to cover several of the law codes. After his conversion to Christianity, Aethelbert of Kent promulgated new laws (*c.* 602), and one of his motives for doing so was a new problem: to provide penalties for offenses against the Church. In Wessex the dooms of King Ine (688–95) were in part again evoked by the needs of the Church, in part by the need to do justice to the Welsh as his kingdom expanded into the territory which they occupied, in part to deal with the growing problems of lordship and economic dependence.[3] Many of King Alfred's laws sprang from the need for more effective enforcement after the collapse which the Danish wars had brought about. The tenth century again had its problems, and it was prolific, indeed, in law codes—with two from Edward the Elder, four from Edgar, and nine or ten from Aethelraed. These were largely promulgated to meet the needs of the Scandinavian settlers and invaders. For the same reason Cnut issued a comprehensive series of laws. Yet most of these later law codes also provided for the more effective enforcement of existing law. On the whole, there was, as one would expect from the still surviving principle of tribal law, less addition to the content of the various regional customary laws involving private relationships and property than to new sanctions for enforcing them.

The monarchy found an almost natural ally in the Church, for the Church could carry on its work most effectively when good order reigned in the land. Churchmen strongly supported royal efforts to see that order pre-

[3] See p. 103.

vailed, and in so doing they stressed the king's position as God's representative on earth, the stern and righteous ruler enforcing internal peace and justice, a semisanctification that made him something more than the traditional leader of the war band.

Early Taxation

As the functions of the state were limited compared with those of modern times, so were its resources. Restricted functions and restricted means obviously interact, while the growth of power and the increase in financial resources go hand in hand. The modern state is financed out of regular taxation, but this was not so in England, or in any other European country, until the seventeenth century. To use a phrase which became popular in the later Middle Ages, the king was expected to "live of his own" and not to call on his subjects to provide him with money by direct taxation, except in grave emergencies. The king's "own" differed somewhat in its scope from time to time, but by and large the Anglo-Saxon kings, like their successors up to the days of the early Stuarts, drew a major part of their revenue from their landed estates—they lived more like private men with fixed incomes than like modern governments which can vary their revenues annually to meet changing needs. In addition, certain types of borough tenants made payments to the king. As he and his household traveled about the countryside supervising the work of government, the districts he visited were obliged to support him, generally with supplies in kind or with levies which, however, were often commuted into money payments.

An income of growing importance lay in the profits of justice, and this source became very significant, indeed, after the Norman Conquest, when the words *Justitia est magnum emolumentum*[4] rose to the status of a proverb. As the idea of the king's "frith," or peace, grew stronger, an increasing number of offenses came to be regarded less as injuries to some individual and more as violations of this special peace. This tendency appeared especially in the efforts of King Alfred's descendants to reestablish good order after the Danish invasions. The monarchy gradually established the exclusive right to "out-law" and "in-law" a man, and from Edward the Elder's (899–925) time kings began to impose "oferhynes," that is, special fines to be paid to the king for disobeying his orders. Such supervision was eventually extended to the proceedings of the popular courts. The functions of kingship and its income were growing together. A new concept was gradually rising, the concept of the peace of the whole community, the concept of crime against the community, in addition to the

---

[4] "Justice is very profitable."

traditional concept of offenses against individuals or kindred groups. However, this later concept did not reach coherent, conscious expression until the time of Henry II (1154–89).

Late Anglo-Saxon England was much more advanced than any other European country in that it had one real tax in the modern sense, the geld.[5] Yet, except for one short period, this tax could not be counted as part of the king's normal revenue. It was first levied in 991 to buy off the Danes with great bribes. Cnut turned it into an annual tax to support his army and fleet, and it continued to be paid until Edward the Confessor abolished it as a regular levy in 1051.

Anglo-Saxon Administration

The late Anglo-Saxon kings also developed a central administrative system. Though advanced in its techniques, it was, in practice, a slight affair. In the conditions of the day it could hardly be anything else. With population thin and transport poor, expensive, and slow, the activities of the central government were inevitably limited. Nevertheless, the institutions of Anglo-Saxon government provided the firmest basis of any in Europe for future development.

The central governments of all Western European countries began in the households of their kings, and officials had names like "chamberlain" and "steward" according to their domestic origins. By the reign of Aethelstan such officials were already sufficiently important to act as witnesses to the royal charters, and by 1066 they were well on their way to being, in part, public officials.

One of the most important organs of government was the king's chamber. This, as the name indicates, was the monarch's private apartment, his bedchamber. Adjacent to it lay the wardrobe, containing not only the king's clothes but the treasure chest which contained his money and important documents like papal bulls. From Cnut's (1016–35) time onward there was also a permanent treasure hoard at Winchester, in its organization an offshoot of the chamber. Domesday Book, a record of a great survey of the country that William the Conqueror ordered to be carried out in 1087, shows beyond doubt that before 1066 there existed an expert financial organization capable of supervising the wites,[6] the moneys due from sheriffs, the tolls, and the geld. Its officials kept accounts and even, by the assay, tested the purity of the silver coins presented to them in payment. The organization was effective enough not only for immediate needs but for those of the generation after the Norman Conquest as well.

---

[5] See p. 104.
[6] Fines imposed for offenses and payable to the king.

The twelfth-century civil servant Richard FitzNeal, in the *Dialogus de Scaccario*,[7] wrote, "When William the Conqueror had subdued the whole island and by terrible examples had tamed the minds of the rebels he decided to place the government of the people on a written basis and subject them to the rule of law (*juri scripto legibusque*)." The attempt to replace mere memory and the spoken word by documents was one of the greatest of all advances in government, representing an enormous development in potentiality, efficiency, and scope. As we shall see later, a very great advance in this direction came at the end of the twelfth century. Meanwhile, the Anglo-Saxon kings had already made use of written instruments in their administration, although it is not possible to say exactly when this began.

The earliest written instruments were land books, or charters. A charter is a solemn document recording a gift or grant. Their issue began early, almost certainly under the influence of churchmen, accustomed to continental practices, who sought the greater certainty of written records for grants of land made for the support of churches and monasteries. There are two main series of charters, the first beginning in the seventh century and coming (for some unknown reason) to an end before the reign of King Alfred. These earlier charters were generally drawn up by the interested parties and presented to the king for ratification when he happened to be available; that is, they were local and occasional products. The later charters, beginning with the reign of King Aethelstan, show an identity of formulae and style that only an organized writing office at the royal court can account for. By Aethelraed's (979–1016) time these charters were being lodged in the royal chapel for safekeeping and for reference. With a royal *scriptorium*, the stock form and the record office came into existence.

Charters, however, were too complicated to be used in day-to-day administration. From the tenth century at the latest a much simpler instrument, the sealed writ, was used—the first surviving examples come from Aethelraed's reign. Far less complicated and less formal than charters, writs were brief informal notifications of what the king had done or of what he wished to be done. Diplomatically ("diplomatic" is the scientific study of the form and composition of original documents), the writ is a very highly developed instrument. It was simple—in complete contrast to the charter or to any other extant document, English or foreign, of the period—and it was written in the vernacular many generations before any other country abandoned Latin for purposes of administration. Although a generation after the Norman Conquest Latin replaced English as the language of the writ, this Anglo-Saxon form remained basic for all royal administrative orders until the sixteenth century.

The king's chaplains were also his clerical staff, and although after

---

[7] "Dialogue of the Exchequer."

the Norman Conquest the chancery developed separately from the chapel, as late as the second half of the twelfth century the chancellor could at times still be regarded only as the most dignified of the royal chaplains. From Cnut's time onward, however, men who began their careers as royal scribes ended as bishops and abbots; a sure sign of their importance.

In spite of these developments, the royal staff was no more than a mere handful of men. Therefore, the king was quite unable to rule directly over most of the countryside. Apart from the customary law administered in the "folk moots,"[8] now and for centuries to come, whether he liked it or not, the king had to rely on the cooperation of the rich, with all the limitations which this necessarily imposed upon him. Government operated through a kind of syndicate of the king and a small agrarian upper class, probably about 2 percent of the adult male population. Their lordship, which we have mentioned earlier, was fundamental to the cohesion and discipline of society. Conflict is always more interesting to read about than the quiet, undramatic course of normal day-to-day administration, and from records of violent clashes and struggles which broke out between them from time to time it is easy to gain the impression that the interests of the kings and the magnates were diametrically opposed—were forever locked in a competitive struggle for power. Nothing could be further from the truth. Neither could really function without the other, and cooperation between king and lords was the normal state of affairs. Only the local territorial aristocracy could give the affairs of their countryside, their own localities, the detailed attention which these demanded, and only a strong personality on the throne could hold a balance of power among the magnates, adjudicate their frequent quarrels, and induce them to devote their energies to the constructive tasks of government rather than to the prosecution of feuds among themselves. The reign of a minor, or a king of less than aggressive and powerful personality, always spelled disaster, not so much because he lost direct control over government offices but because he forfeited the respect of the powerful aristocracy.

Anglo-Saxon Social Structure

Anglo-Saxon society was always far from egalitarian. From the beginning it was unequal, and as time went on it became more so.[9] The "wergild"[10] of a "ceorl"[11] in Wessex was 200 shillings; that of a noble, 1,200. Other distinctions sprang from a man's official position as well as blood. If, for

---

[8] Popular assemblies.
[9] See pp. 103–05.
[10] The sum paid in compensation to the kin of a slain man.
[11] A free man, but below noble rank.

example, a king's thegn was accused of any offense, he was to be cleared by the oaths of twelve other king's thegns, by the assistance of his equals, not of his social inferiors. At the same time, the nobility was not a closed caste. Anglo-Saxon and medieval England were always highly realistic about status. Power and high status in the community were always the by-product of wealth. Indeed, a poor nobleman was almost a contradiction in terms. A ceorl who acquired enough land and a merchant who "fared thrice over the wide sea by his own means" could become thegns, and if a thegn throve to sufficient wealth he could become an earl.[12]

The meaning of thegn was "one who serves another." In origin, the thegnship was a nobility of service, not of blood, although the thegn was, generally speaking, a retainer of noble birth to whom it became customary to grant estates in return for service. By Cnut's time, in the popular mind the typical thegn was a man with specific duties in the royal household who possessed an estate sufficient for the support of at least twenty peasant families. As there was no district law of succession, however, the class seems to have been highly fluid. Some thegns divided their holdings among several sons, who thereby sank in the social scale. Others accumulated estates over several generations and became extremely rich. One of them, Wulfric Spot, who flourished about the year 1000, founded Burton Abbey and in his will disposed of land in more than seventy villages in northern Mercia and southern Northumbria.

When the West Saxon monarchy had imposed the shire and the hundred on the country, it had also to devise methods of keeping in touch with them. One of these methods was the institution of the sheriff, who in time became the monarchy's chief executive in the shire, collected revenues from the royal estates, presided over the shire courts, and, mainly through deputies, also presided over the more frequent sessions of the hundred courts. The thegns, however, were also a link between the central government and the local divisions. In King Alfred's time, at least, the king's thegns, filling the most important offices in rotation, attended court periodically and spent the rest of their time on their estates. This method of contact lasted for centuries. The Household Ordinances of Edward IV (1461–83) also reveal that his knights and esquires of the body did turn and turn about, three months at a time, at court and in the countryside. The thegns thus helped to keep the king in touch with the shires, and he also used them for any occasional business in which he had a personal interest.

At the head of this social hierarchy were the ealdormen—during and after Cnut's time they became known instead by the Scandinavian title

---

[12] See pp. 59–60.

"earl." Their power was based on both land and office. Although, by the standards of the day, they were men of such great landed wealth (generally scattered through many shires) that no king could possibly afford to ignore them, they never established a strictly hereditary position upon which, like continental magnates, they assumed control of entire provinces. The king always appointed them to their offices, and the boundaries of their earldoms, far from coinciding with their personal estates, were frequently changed and reorganized at the king's will. There was, however, a natural tendency for the rank, if not the bailiwick, to become hereditary. By the middle of the Confessor's reign there were three principal comital[13] families, associated with the names of Godwin, Leofric, and Siward: all three of them men whom Cnut had quite recently promoted to the rank of earl. The ambitions of Godwin's family account in great degree for the political tensions at the court of Edward the Confessor (1042–66). Some historians have claimed that the growing power of these comital families was steadily eroding the powers of the Old English monarchy in the last years before the Norman Conquest—that the monarchy's great potential legal and administrative strength was weakening before the nobility's might. Nevertheless, we must not exaggerate this tendency: in a crisis the last word generally lay with King Edward. It was a royal grant that gave an earl his authority; the principle that an earl brought in by revolution must be confirmed in office by the king was recognized even in the wildest parts of the country, those most remote from the court. In 1065 the Northumbrians drove out their earl, Godwin's son Tostig, and chose in his place Morcar, the brother of the Earl of Mercia, and King Edward's last public act was to grant their request that Morcar should be their earl. It was all a strange mixture of local consciousness and the idea of allegiance to the central authority.

An institution which helped to knit the country more closely together was the Witan, a kind of royal council of prominent men. The itineraries of King Aethelstan show that his interests were still mainly in the South, that he rarely traveled outside the borders of the old West Saxon Kingdom but he established greater contact with the remoter parts of the kingdom by inducing the magnates to attend him in the South. For example, on March 23, 931, in a Witan at Colchester, there were at least thirty-seven thegns, thirteen earls, of whom six were Danes, three abbots, fifteen bishops, and the Archbishop of Canterbury. As a result of this development, prominent men from all parts of the country, not merely from Wessex as formerly, attended the royal councils and gave their advice on government policy, a practice that did a good deal to break down local separatism.

All the same, we must be on our guard against giving too great an air of modernity to all this. Although the late Anglo-Saxon state had to its credit administrative achievements more solid than any in Europe, efficiency

---

[13] Families of earls, derived from *comte*, the French equivalent of the English "earl."

and justice are relative conceptions which grow parallel in power and refinement to the financial and administrative resources of the state. As we have seen, the resources of the Anglo-Saxon monarchy were far too meager to allow its own officers to interfere in the day-to-day affairs of the countryside. At most, they could exercise supervision over the local assemblies. Even in matters of justice, the king (alone or in the Witan) dealt only with the cases of the greatest men, offenses which were committed within the precincts of the court itself and perhaps in those districts where the king happened to travel. Even the use of the writ, it has been suggested, was no more than potential, to be developed on a greater scale only in the two generations after the Norman Conquest.

Corruption and violence were everywhere and at all times the curse of social relationships. The corollary of *Justitia est magnum emolumentum* was that justice could be bought. As late as the reign of Henry VII, and even later, English kings accepted gifts from their subjects in return for favors shown in judicial matters, and the influence of king and magnates rather than their technical merits before the law decided a good many cases. Another major defect was that in a society where the state could afford neither a police force nor a standing army the procedures of justice were, themselves, more than tinged with violence. Alfred's laws allowed an injured man "to surround his adversary and besiege him in his house" for seven days in order to make him submit to justice, and the king obviously thought this procedure a great improvement on existing practice, for the same law forbade violence against the person of the offender. In spite of the development of lordship, the kindred still pursued the vendetta: the principle that the family of a slain man must inflict vengeance in kind on the family of the slayer. Although regulated and restricted by complicated rules, the vendetta was still horribly wasteful of human life. Punishment partook of the same taint. In 1051 when the burgesses of Dover had fallen into a brawl with the men of Count Eustace of Boulogne, the supposedly gentle and saintly Edward the Confessor commanded their lord, Earl Godwin, to harry the town—that is, to take in a gang of strong-arm boys and beat up the inhabitants. Such government by punitive expedition can hardly be called a very sophisticated form of control.

On the eve of the Norman Conquest England was still, in many ways, a primitive society. Yet, within limits, the monarchy had developed such control over the countryside that, with the possible exception of Ottonian Germany, England was the strongest state in Europe. It had proved itself capable of overcoming the inertia inherent in tradition-bound local communities and institutions. The personality of the reigning king had always been, and for long afterwards remained, the force in the land that stimulated change and innovation.

CHAPTER FOUR

The Norman Conquest

As the Anglo-Saxons had developed what was for the times a well-knit, well-governed state, it may at first seem surprising that they failed to repel William, Duke of Normandy, when he landed at Pevensey on September 28, 1066, with a heterogeneous army of about 5,000 men recruited from half a dozen French provinces. William's success can in no way be attributed to any superiority in the institutions of the duchy of Normandy. He owed his narrowly won victory to a temporary combination of circumstances adverse to King Harold of England—and to the weather. What little we know of Normandy before 1066 indicates a state less advanced than Anglo-Saxon England. It was, moreover, a different type of state—Duke William, born a bastard and succeeding as a minor (both considerable obstacles to successful government) had, after great struggles, established his power on the basis of an aristocracy of very recent origin, the greater among them connected by marriage with the ducal family, and some of them endowed with estates from the ducal lands. Both William and his followers were greedy and aggressive; like other European rulers, William was trying

The Norman Conquest
and
Anglo-Norman Government

to build up a feudal[1] society and was competing for vassals. Some of the greater families of Normandy, attracted by opportunities there, had come from outside the duchy—from France, from Brittany, even from Germany: aggressive families who expected a vigorous leader to wage campaigns for profit. England by that time was a rich country, probably already wealthy from wool production, which later brought many of its inhabitants great prosperity and, in the fourteenth century, enabled its kings to wage prolonged warfare against France, a much larger and wealthier country. Given a favorable opportunity, the Normans found it a natural objective for expansion as had the Saxons and Danes earlier.

In 1066 the opportunity came. William's continental neighbors—France, Flanders, and Anjou—were all, by a fortunate coincidence, in no position to oppose his plans. He had a claim of sorts to the English throne: he was the cousin of Edward the Confessor, who had died childless and who, sometime in 1051–52, had promised William the English throne. Norman propaganda after 1066 stressed the sanctity of this promise very

---

[1] William never, of course, used the word "feudal" himself. It was introduced only in the seventeenth century.

Bayeux Tapestry, commissioned by Bishop Odo of Bayeux, *c.* 1077. *Top left:* Harold's coronation; *right:* A comet is sighted, which Harold regards as a bad omen. *Bottom:* Harold (*at left*) is struck down and killed at Hastings by a Norman knight while the remainder of Harold's army collapses. (*Top:* Giraudon; *bottom:* from *The Bayeux Tapestry,* Phaidon Press, London.)

heavily indeed, but it may well be doubtful whether it had been more than a temporary move in a very complicated, but now exceedingly obscure, diplomatic game. Earl Godwin's son Harold, at some disputed date, had also given William his oath that he would support this claim. But just before Edward the Confessor died he designated Harold as his successor, thus, according to the Norman chroniclers at least, going back on his promise to the duke. Harold was accepted by the Witan, broke his own oath, and took the throne.

Unfortunately for Harold, his family was unruly and tempestuous.

One brother Sweyn (by this time dead) had been forced to go on pilgrimage barefoot to Jerusalem as a penance for the murder of his cousin, Earl Beorn. The youngest brother, Tostig, had been Earl of Northumbria until his haughty temperament and somewhat rough justice provoked a revolt against him in 1065. Harold concurred with the king in depriving Tostig of his earldom. Tostig, vowing vengeance, fled to solicit help from the King of Norway, the renowned warrior Harold Hardrada, who immediately fell in with his plans. By the summer of 1066, therefore, England had to face the double threat of invasions from both Norway and Normandy. Both invasions came to pass, and in less than a month the English were forced to fight three pitched battles, of which Hastings against the Normans was only the last. Harold Hardrada and Tostig invaded through the Humber and defeated the earls Edwin and Morcar at Fulford on September 20. Harold, rapidly marching north, five days later in turn inflicted a crushing defeat on the invaders at Stamford Bridge, only to hear, again within a few days, of the Norman landing at Pevensey.

William had assembled a distinctly motley army. Many of his vassals had grave doubts about the wisdom of the enterprise, and as they recognized no obligation to serve overseas the feudal host of Normandy could not be called out en masse. Norman vassals joined William only in return for bribes and promises of a share in the plunder. Adventurers from Brittany, Flanders, Aquitaine, and even southern Italy came to him on the same terms, possibly encouraged by the success with which the Norman family of Hauteville had recently won themselves a principality in Apulia and Calabria.

William now faced circumstances over which he had no control. Five thousand men, of whom nearly a half were knights, waited with their horses for transport across the channel. They waited through an entire month of adverse winds until the southerly wind of the equinox carried them to Pevensey on September 28. If the wind had changed earlier, William would have found the English fully prepared, ready to repel his landing—which King Harold was convinced that they could do. If, on the other hand, the change of wind had been much longer delayed, William, who had already worked wonders in controlling and feeding his composite host, could hardly have kept it together.

After Fulford and Stamford Bridge, King Harold had to march 250 miles south. Many of his soldiers were unable to withstand the strain of these long, forced marches, and on October 14 at Hastings Harold faced the Normans with tired and depleted forces. Even so, one of the Norman host, Robert FitzWimarc, begged the duke to return to Normandy because, in comparison with the mighty English army which was approaching, the Normans appeared to him to be "so many despicable dogs." The Normans were victorious after six hours hard fighting only as the result of a stratagem, a feigned flight which lured the English to break their ranks in pursuit. The Norman Conquest, universally recognized as one of the major turning points of English history, had nothing inevitable about it.

The Norman Occupation
and the Feudal System

As R. H. C. Davis has recently remarked,[2] countries which are well governed should be able to resist invading armies more surely than countries which are not, but if they fail their efficient governmental systems make them easier for their conquerors to control. This dictum was certainly the case in England in 1066. King Harold's death at Hastings left no rallying point for Anglo-Saxon resistance. Although in certain districts resistance was fierce, it was disorganized and piecemeal rather than concerted. Nor was the reaction of the populace what it would be today. As we have seen, the population was a mixture: part Anglo-Saxon, part Danish. By blood the Danes were closer to the Normans than to the Anglo-Saxons, for the Norman upper classes were themselves mostly of Danish extraction. On the whole, the populace was not unwilling to submit to a new ruler if he was capable of giving them firm government.

Though some historians have seen William's 5,000 adventurers as an army of occupation holding down a sullen countryside, the situation was more complicated. As early as 1068 the Anglo-Saxon "fyrd" cooperated with William in quelling a native revolt in Exeter, and it later fought with him in France and against his rebellious Norman vassals. Moreover, no one at the time had the power to transform the whole range of government by the introduction of completely new institutions. Therefore, partly out of necessity, partly to win over the English, partly to exploit existing royal powers to their fullest limit, William chose to regard himself as the natural, legitimate successor to the English kings. The Witan recognized his title, and he was crowned with the English coronation rite. Early in 1067 he granted the city of London a charter (written in Anglo-Saxon) confirming all its traditional privileges. Thus, as it guaranteed their rights, numbers of Englishmen came to have a vested interest in the new monarchy. As the king left the system of local government—the shire and the hundred courts —intact, their rights, and those which the Norman newcomers acquired, were guaranteed by the law and by the same procedures as in Anglo-Saxon times.

Such continuity is well illustrated by an incident which occurred in 1075 or 1076. No invasion, after all, could take place without considerable disturbance to individual property rights, and there is ample evidence that in the confusion of the immediate postconquest years lawless elements laid hold of lands to which they had no legal rights. In many cases the lands

[2] *History*, L (1966).

of the Church were thus unjustly seized. A conflict of this kind arose between William's able, but avaricious and unscrupulous, half-brother, Odo, whom he had made Earl of Kent, and Lanfranc, the Norman Archbishop of Canterbury. Lanfranc applied to the king for a royal enquiry to settle the matter. William issued a writ, an Anglo-Saxon instrument, ordering an inquest to be held in the shire court of Kent. It commanded all people who knew anything about the matter, French or English, but especially all Englishmen who were learned in the law, to attend the court on Penenden Heath. The enquiry there lasted for three days and reviewed all the rights and liberties of Lanfranc's church. The whole shire court "stood for record" (bore witness to) as it would have done in Anglo-Saxon times. At every point appeal was made to Old English practice and to individuals familiar with it. By the king's own orders, the aged bishop Aethelric of Selsey was brought to the meeting in a cart (a luxurious concession to the infirmities of old age) in order to answer the questions of Anglo-Saxon law that were expected to arise. The incident is a perfect example of the king's wish to maintain institutional continuity.

At the same time William took every advantage of the strategic fact that he had won the throne by conquest at the head of an army which had followed him in the expectation of great rewards. The Anglo-Saxon aristocracy was largely destroyed in the fighting of 1066, and over the next few years the king expropriated what was left of it until there remained barely half a dozen Anglo-Saxon landowners of any substance. The Norman Conquest saw the greatest change in landownership in English history. The change also brought about a fundamental change in the nature of landholding: the introduction of feudalism, which replaced Anglo-Saxon land law by a new type of relationship between the land and its occupants. The thegns of Anglo-Saxon England owed their king or lord military service in their personal capacity, not in respect of their estates. The Conqueror now introduced the radical, foreign conception of military service based on dependent tenure—military service in return for a fee or fief.

William began from the principle that the king had become, by conquest, the absolute owner of all the land in the kingdom—a principle the Anglo-Saxon kings had never been able to establish. He granted estates to other men to hold conditionally in return for well-defined services. He kept enough land in his own hands to double the income which Edward the Confessor had received from the royal estates. With the remainder, by about 1070, he made arrangements for the support of a professional army of about 5,000 mounted knights of the kind who were to dominate warfare until the rise of the archer in the late thirteenth and early fourteenth centuries. The organization of this army and the reward of his followers were now tied together. The king rewarded his more powerful men with the estates of the vanished Anglo-Saxon aristocracy: the estates, about 180 in all, now came to be known as "baronies." These men, known as tenants-in-chief, holding land directly from the king, were obliged to provide an agreed number of knights for his armies at their own expense. They then faced the problem of organizing these contingents. As far as we can see, William concerned himself very little with this second stage. He had neither the information on which to do so, nor probably the inclination to interfere.

At first the tenants-in-chief supported knights in their own households. Many, however, especially bishops and abbots who also had this military obligation imposed on them for their estates, found it inconvenient, to say the least, to be at such constant close quarters with swaggering gangs of prizefighters. They, therefore, adopted the plan of settling their knights on the land in return for military service. Knights settled in this way were known as *"subtenants"* or *"undertenants,"* and the process as *"subinfeudation."* The knights bore the same relationship to their lords as their lords bore to the king. The whole process at all its stages was far from uniform; in fact, it was distinctly haphazard. Orderic Vitalis (1075–c. 1142) tells us that while some Norman tenants-in-chief found themselves with lands rich beyond expectation, others complained that they had been given barren farms and domains depopulated by war. As late as 1135, subinfeudation was by no means complete, and many tenants-in-chief still supported some of their knights on the "demesne"[3] rather than by giving them land. Some made the best of adverse circumstances by allowing men who had illegally seized lands during the troubled years immediately after the Conquest to keep them in return for military services. The Abbey of Ely, which had suffered badly from such predatory activities, provided seventeen out of its quota of forty knights in this way.

The land on which a single knight was settled in return for military service came to be known as a "knight's fee." The fee was not a uniform amount of land. In the immediate postconquest period, it varied greatly in size and value—some of the Archbishop of Canterbury's knights were little more than well-to-do peasants. By the mid-twelfth century, however, there was a tendency to consider that a knight's fee should be an estate giving an income of about £20 a year.[4]

Until recently the military significance, as distinct from the long-term social effects of the Norman changes, has been very much overestimated. The feudal quotas by no means provided the whole of the Anglo-Norman military forces; William and both his sons made considerable use of the Anglo-Saxon fyrd. Moreover, feudalism had originally developed in Europe at a time when the economy had sunk to such a very low level that it was

---

[3] That part of his estate which a lord exploited directly, as distinct from his leasing or granting it to subtenants.
[4] Twenty pounds a year placed a man in the upper classes. Eight pence a day was the pay of a mercenary knight; twelve or thirteen shillings a year the wages of a plowman.

almost impossible to support cavalry except by endowing soldiers with land. By the time of the Norman Conquest, the European economy had already revived, and judging from the proceeds of the geld,[5] England could provide its rulers, even if only intermittently, with very considerable cash revenues. The Anglo-Norman kings spent part of these revenues to hire large numbers of foreign mercenaries, both for the defense of England itself and for their continental wars. For example, in 1103 Henry I made the Treaty of Dover with Count Robert of Flanders. In return for an annual pension of £500, Robert agreed to provide 1,000 knights for service in Normandy or 500 in Maine. It is surely significant that when the whole feudal service of England produced no more than 5,000 knights Henry should have arranged for the service of 1,000 from one external source alone. England's military arrangements were not so completely feudal as historians have sometimes claimed.

The greater feudal estates came to be called *"honors."* These were far more than a mere collection of lands, and in the long run their functions were more significant than the immediate provision of military service. Yet the history of the honor is, unfortunately, one of the most obscure subjects in the whole of English development. The shire and the hundred have a long, living history, for the shire is, after all, still the basic unit of English administration. But the honor as a vital unit lasted less than two centuries, and its life is difficult to reconstruct. The honor was a group of estates, which might be scattered anywhere over England, that were held in feudal tenure from the king by a single lord, who controlled it as a single unit. In many ways, the honor was a smaller edition of the feudal aspects of the royal government. It applied only to those people, the subtenants, who held land by military service. It did not directly touch the peasants or men who held by other forms of tenure. Just as the tenants-in-chief were expected to attend the royal court, especially at the three great formal crown wearings of the year—Christmas, Easter, and Whitsuntide[6]—the tenant-in-chief expected his own vassals to attend his honorial court and council, to give advice about the affairs and administration of the honor, and to assist in giving judgments against their fellows who contravened its customs or who withheld their due services from the lord.

Although details are rare, it seems true that the administrative and consultative functions that the feudal subtenants performed within the honors formed a most valuable administrative and political training that contributed a great deal to the steady development of political life. The habits of cooperation and discussion there formed and the definitions of feudal jurisprudence that evolved in the individual honorial courts were gradually incorporated by the central government into political life on a national scale. Today experience in local government is often a valuable

---

[5] See pp. 88, 104.
[6] The feast of the Church that falls seven weeks after Easter.

preliminary to national political office, and this was true of the honor in the eleventh and twelfth centuries. The procedures and habits which evolved in the honors made a great contribution to the development of the national courts by Henry II and his successors.

The Norman Kings and Government

In spite of its achievements, the Anglo-Norman period was an era of instability and violence. This violence was partly endemic in the limited scope and powers of government at the time, partly due to the upheaval caused by the conquest itself, and partly due to the type of men that William employed.

As we have seen, when allocating land to his followers William simply did not know its value. Nor was he very certain of some of his own fiscal rights. Moreover, as the grants were vague (generally being the estates of some dead Anglo-Saxon), the grantees generally had to establish the boundaries themselves, and they seem to have done so by inquests in the shire courts. Others took the opportunity to seize lands illegitimately. Over the years there were numerous complaints of injustice and a number of prominent lawsuits. In 1086, therefore, for a number of reasons—to ascertain in detail his rights to the geld, to estimate the country's military resources in order to repel a threatened invasion from Scandinavia, to bring order into the confusion of conflicting tenures—William ordered a great survey of the country to be carried out. The results, digested and written into the famous Domesday Book, represent an administrative achievement unparalleled in contemporary Europe. Nothing like it was seen again in England until Henry VIII commissioned the *Valor Ecclesiasticus*, a minute survey of all Church property in the country. As the Anglo-Saxon *Chronicle* indignantly wrote, "It is shame to tell though he thought no shame to do it. So very narrowly he caused it to be traced out that there was not one single hide or yard of land, not even an ox, nor a cow, nor a swine, that was not set down in writing." Every Norman was forced to account for the way in which he had acquired his English lands.[7] Domesday Book chronicled the results of the Norman Conquest by examining the details of its resulting land settlement, approving them or rejecting them: that is how it received its name—the great book of judgments.

Yet, in spite of Domesday Book, William the Conqueror was a man of brutal, ruthless energy rather than a constructive genius. He had won his position in Normandy by grim tenacity against appalling odds, and in England he proved capable of quelling revolt by terrible devastation of the countryside. After his campaign of 1069 not a single inhabited place remained between York and Durham—though in justice it should be remem-

[7] R. H. C. Davis, *History*, li (1966).

bered that King Harold had been capable of almost equal ferocity. There is no evidence that William did much to develop new institutions of government in Normandy, and, as we have seen, after 1066 he was content to take over the superior institutions of Anglo-Saxon England. He was grim and tenacious enough to be successful, and he dealt out a rough, stern justice that impressed a salutary fear upon his subjects. The best character sketch of the king is to be found in the Anglo-Saxon *Chronicle*, whose author, a member of a conquered race, had no particular cause to love him but could not withhold a certain grudging admiration:

> This King William then that we speak about was a very wise man, and very rich; more splendid and more powerful than any of his predecessors were. He was mild to the good men that loved God,[8] and beyond all measure severe to the men that gainsaid his will. . . . So very stern was he also and hot, that no man durst do anything against his will. He had earls in his custody, who acted against his will. Bishops he hurled from their bishoprics, and abbots from their abbacies and thegns into prison. At length he spared not his own brother, Odo. . . . But amongst other things is not to be forgotten that good peace that he made in this land; so that a man of any account might go over his kingdom unhurt with his bosom full of gold. No man durst slay another, had he never so much evil done to the other: and if any churl lay with a woman against her will he soon lost a limb that he played with. He truly reigned over England.

But the *Chronicle* added:

> Assuredly in his time men had much distress and very many sorrows. Castles he let men build and miserably swink the poor. The king himself was so very rigid; and extorted from his subjects many hundred pounds of silver; which he took of his people, for little need, by right and unright. He was fallen into covetousness, and greediness he loved withal. . . .

A harsh fiscality and much oppression undoubtedly marred the firm government of the Conqueror and his two sons. William found it necessary to appoint local men, generally feudal barons, as sheriffs: men strong enough to hold their own in the shires without help from the central government. Though immediately advantageous, the tenure of office by such powerful magnates inevitably led to abuses. While throughout the Middle Ages local officials, from whatever class they came, tended to corruption, the baronial sheriffs of these years had exceptional opportunities to enrich themselves at the expense of other people. Such a man was Picot, the notorious sheriff of Cambridge, a landholder in twenty-two Cambridgeshire villages and prominent enough to attend the Curia Regis.[9] At the time of Domesday Book local jurors accused Picot, among other things, of extorting new labor services and gifts of money, and he was involved in a very

---

[8] The author was a monk, and William was lavish in his endowment of monasteries.
[9] The king's court: the ceremonial, social, and administrative center of the kingdom.

questionable lawsuit against the Bishop of Ely. Picot was a typical post-conquest sheriff: powerful and loyal, but brutal and tyrannical and most unpopular. There was a distinct danger that under such circumstances the sheriffdoms would become hereditary, that sheriffs would become part of the feudal hierarchy instead of appointed officials, and that the king would find his hold over the countryside seriously weakened. In Wiltshire, for example, this did happen: the earls of Salisbury, father to son, succeeding each other as sheriffs. Under Henry I they insisted that the office was hereditary, and their claim was not finally quashed until the days of Henry III (1216–72).

Once the difficulties of the postconquest period had passed, the Conqueror's sons, William Rufus (1087–1100) and Henry I (1100–35), began to extricate the countryside from this feudal monopoly. Rufus appointed special county "justiciars"[10] to take over the greater judicial pleas from the sheriffs, and before 1100 at least two sheriffs in office, Osbert the Priest and Hugh of Buckland, were landless men who owed their position to the crown alone. By 1110 about sixteen shires were held in this way. As usually happens, vested interests greeted these reforms with cries of rage that unworthy men raised from the dust had usurped the traditional aristocratic right to counsel the king and had taken over positions appropriate only for nobles. Yet, in an equally characteristic way, such families as the Clintons and the Bassets, who now, for the first time, appeared in office, in their turn were the founders of noble families.

This new policy in the countryside ran parallel with, and probably reflected, new developments at the center of government: developments stimulated by financial needs; above all, money to pay for the employment of mercenaries. William Rufus's reputation for avarice became even more notorious than his father's, and there is no doubt that he and his chief minister, Ranulf Flambard, acted in a most oppressive way toward the tenants-in-chief. The hereditary principle was not yet fully established.[11] The feudal contract was vague and ill-defined, and Rufus made the most of its vagueness to his own advantage. On the deaths of tenants-in-chief, he exacted enormous "reliefs"[12] before allowing their eldest sons to succeed to their baronies. He left bishoprics and abbacies vacant so that he could enjoy their revenues over long periods.

When Henry I came to the throne in 1100, he issued a coronation charter in which, by implication, he stigmatized his brother's acts as violations of good practice and promised amendment. New administrative developments, however, gave him more efficient means to do as well, or as badly, as his dead brother. As remarked earlier, the government of all Western European states began in the king's household. As the needs of government grew greater, this unitary institution became insufficient, for

---

[10] Officials specially appointed to hear and determine legal cases.
[11] See pp. 75–77.
[12] A sum of money payable by the heir upon succession to a military fief.

new tasks demanded special skills. In a writ of 1110 a new word appears—Exchequer (*Scaccarium*), best described as the Curia Regis in its financial aspect. At first the Curia Regis set aside special sessions or occasions for the transaction of particular types of business; somewhat later, it threw off specialized institutions which, as the phrase ran, went "out of court." Such institutions ultimately developed their own techniques of conducting business and their own staffs. These new "civil servants" (although, of course, they were not yet called by this name: the term did not appear until the end of the eighteenth century) developed a loyalty both to the king and to their departments quite distinct from—even, at times, opposed to—the loyalties of feudalism.

The Exchequer at this time was in its first stage of development, for it did not yet limit itself entirely to financial matters. There was not a single function of government which it did not perform, be it financial, judicial, administrative, or deliberative. It was the *Curia Regis ad Scaccarium*, the king's court at the Exchequer. But its main and specialized work was to centralize the financial system, especially the accounting, which up to this time had been dealt with in a somewhat haphazard way. Therefore, special sessions of the *Curia Regis ad Scaccarium* began to be held at Easter and Michaelmas[13] for one purpose only: the king's finances and his bookkeeping. The name "Exchequer," however, derived from the method of accounting introduced with a new department, the Exchequer of Account (also known as the Upper Exchequer), a revolutionary system of reckoning with counters on an abacus, or on a "chequered" table. This system was an Arabian device imported from Sicily, perhaps via northern France. Aids of this kind for arithmetic were essential at a time when all calculations were made in Roman numerals. The collection of revenue was probably not much in advance of Anglo-Saxon practice. The sheriffs still collected money locally, brought it into headquarters, and paid it into the treasury as before. The treasury soon adopted the alternative titles of Lower Exchequer or Exchequer of Receipt. The results of the Exchequer audit and other decisions were carefully recorded in the Pipe Rolls;[14] the first to survive is the roll for 1130–31. In a primitive form, the specialized government department with a location of its own had come into being, as had, for the first time, with the Pipe Roll, the most important technique of keeping a continuous government record with all that such a thing implies in the way of greater convenience, more accurate checks on subordinate officials, and better memory.

This development towards greater efficiency had a murky side. Contemporary and near-contemporary chroniclers unequivocally asserted that Henry went back upon the promises of his coronation oath. It would be unwise to rely upon their unsupported condemnation of the king's methods

[13] The feast of St. Michael, celebrated on September 29.
[14] Probably so called because the accounts on parchment were kept rolled up in the form of a pipe.

and of his *novi homines* or "new men," for these captious writers were monks born of feudal families, representing the outlook and the prejudices of the feudal world, and their monasteries were feudal tenants very much affected by the king's actions. People with strong vested interests always make very loud noises about governmental innovations which hit their pockets. In this case, however, there is a good deal of supporting evidence. All men accepted the fact that *Justitia est magnum emolumentum*, but the lengths to which Henry went in pursuit of gain revolted even one of his own justices, who complained that:

> Law varies through the counties as the avarice and the sinister, odious activity of legal experts adds more grievous means of injury to established legal process. There is so much perversity and such affluence of evil that the certain truth of law and the remedy established by settled provision can rarely be found, but to the great confusion of all a new method of impleading is sought out, a new subtlety of injury is found, as if that which was before hurt little, and he is thought of most account who does most harm to most people, and whatever does not agree with our cruelty does not exist for us. We assume the character of tyrants and it is desire of wealth which brings this madness upon us. . . .[15]

The amounts of the fines recorded on the Pipe Roll bear out these accusations. Although more subtle, Henry was as greedy as William Rufus had been. He carried his business methods beyond the limits of decency, not from mere thoughtless tyranny but from conscious policy. It was little wonder that he had the reputation of being the richest king in Christendom. Henry I had driven matters so far beyond what the public opinion of his day was prepared to allow that, even had his death not been followed by a disputed succession, there would probably have been a feudal revolt.

Matilda and Stephen: Feudal Revolt and the Hereditary System

There was still no definite law governing the descent of the Crown: the really vital factor was the agreement and consent of the great men. On Henry I's death his daughter Matilda and his nephew Stephen, Count of Mortain, both claimed the throne. Although the magnates recognized Stephen, Matilda, with the aid of various discontented barons, was able to dispute his possession of the kingdom for many years, and the country knew the horrors of civil war. The nineteen years of Stephen's reign were a period of retreat for the monarchy. Its treatment of some of the great magnates as well as its harsh fiscality had provoked bitter resentment, and

---

[15] *Leges Henrici Primi*, 6, 3a–b, 6. Translated and quoted in F. M. Stenton, *The First Century of English Feudalism, 1066–1166* (2nd ed.; London, 1961), p. 220.

another fundamental aspect of Anglo-Norman government was now successfully challenged: the deliberately maintained fluidity of landholding.

The principle of hereditary succession, which for centuries has been so vital and so basic an aspect of European culture, was not yet firmly established. Like the succession to the Crown itself, the succession to many estates, based upon no firmly recognized principle, was confused and uncertain. Thus many knight's fees were unstable. When a tenant died, the contract of land in return for military service was automatically broken. It was then imperative for the lord to arrange for the military service due from the fief to be performed as soon as possible, and generally a renewal of the contract with the dead man's eldest son was the easiest way, although the tenants' natural desire to transform the fief into a permanent endowment for their families powerfully stimulated this tendency. Custom hardened into law, and during the early twelfth century the fief became hereditary.

The position of the greater tenants-in-chief was more complicated and politically far more dangerous. William the Conqueror and his sons seem, quite deliberately, to have granted many estates at their pleasure rather than in perpetuity. If the magnates proved insubordinate, they expected to keep a firmer control over them with the threat of deprivation. By means of questionable forfeitures and escheats,[16] they had deprived important families of their estates and had given them to "new men" bound to the king by immediate ties of self-interest. Thus there were always a number of disgruntled families who considered themselves disinherited, so that, among other things, one of the aims of the baronial reaction was to establish the hereditary principle. It may well be that in the end the system which the Anglo-Norman kings had created led almost inevitably to civil war.

Stephen's reign has an evil reputation. Under the year 1137 the Peterborough *Chronicle* records:

> Every rich man built his castles and held them against him: and they filled the land full of castles . . . and this lasted the nineteen winters while Stephen was king, and it grew continually worse and worse . . . they plundered and burned all the towns; so that you could even walk a whole day's journey without finding a man seated in a town or the lands tilled. Then was corn [grain] dear and flesh and cheese and butter for there was none in the land. Wretched men starved of hunger. Some sought alms who had at one time been rich; some fled out of the country. Never was there more misery . . . the earth bore no corn; you might as well have tilled the sea, for the land was all ruined by such deeds; and they said openly that Christ slept and his saints.

Conditions were not everywhere, or over the entire period, as appalling as the chronicler made out. At the beginning of 1148 Matilda left England, and the last five years of Stephen's reign were years of compara-

---

[16] Failure to perform the services or failure of the direct line of succession involved "escheat," that is, the return of the land to the lord.

tive peace, although he never controlled the whole country. The war had been localized, and the Peterborough chronicler lived in a district that had been exceptionally badly ravaged by the notorious Geoffrey de Mandeville.[17] Moreover, several developments tell strongly against any idea of universal degradation. Archbishop Theobald of Canterbury's household was a brilliant center of education, and the Italian lawyer, Vacarius, lectured on Roman law to students at Oxford, the first lectures on this subject ever to be given there. It was also a period of great expansion for the Cistercian order in England: between 1138 and 1152, no less than forty new abbeys were founded and endowed.

But leaving out of account the extent and intensity of the devastations as probably being, in the present state of our knowledge, an insoluble problem, they were bad enough to provoke strong reactions. Men who, in their time, had detested the tyrannies and financial exactions of Henry I, found the conditions of Stephen's reign even worse: in their present wretchedness many came to regard Henry and his justice as something to look back upon almost with regret. In fact, one writer, Henry of Huntingdon,[18] admitted that the idealization of Henry I, which developed during these years, was due to comparison with the widespread misery which came about under his successor.

Very soon the feudal classes themselves began to realize that very few people really profited from weak kingship. For most, in the end, it meant the devastation of at least some of their estates and the destruction of valuable material resources and revenues. In the early years of the civil war the earls of Chester and Leicester even made a treaty with each other, defining their spheres of local influence and the conditions under which either might make war on the other side. Once this had happened, it could hardly be long before men began to recognize the value of law and order and to realize that they could return to peaceful conditions only by submission to a rightful king.

So at Stephen's death the monarchy returned to the strict hereditary line—to Matilda's son Henry of Anjou—but it was a restoration with a difference. Henry II (1154–89), either through policy or timidity, never resumed the excessive financial exactions of his grandfather. The Pipe Rolls show that his gross income during the second year of his reign was slightly less than one-third[19] of Henry I's and, even at the end of his reign (the figures are incomplete), it never consistently reached its former level—and this in a period of greater prosperity and rapidly rising prices.

More explicit, however, was the adoption of the hereditary principle for the Crown's tenants-in-chief. Stephen's elder son had died before his

---

[17] Earl of Essex, who changed sides three times during the civil war and was especially notorious for his treachery, greed, and cruelty.

[18] Born about 1080–90, died sometime after 1154.

[19] This low figure may, of course, be partly due to the fact that it took some time to establish firm control over the country.

father, and Henry II was the man with the best hereditary claim. Moreover, the Treaty of Winchester (1153) between the contending factions, which recognized Henry's claim, also provided that "the disinherited should be restored to their own." The hereditary principle was finally established in the English feudal world. In the twentieth century such emphasis on the accident of birth may seem to many people the ultimate negation of efficiency in government. To the men of the twelfth century it was a practical and progressive reform with the prospect of peace and stability instead of endemic uncertainty and disputes.

The hereditary principle also, if somewhat vaguely, marked an important step in the creation of the higher nobility who were so important in government and policy-making until the late nineteenth century. The principle, if not the treaty, was equally important for the development of the minor nobility or, as they have traditionally been called, the gentry. Many of the original "Norman" knights had been little more than military adventurers and mercenaries, crude thugs who had come to England for the sake of substantial plunder as well as the pickings to be had. The feudal army which they formed proved, from the military point of view, to be an increasingly ineffective, and fleeting, device. It was significant for little more than two centuries. By the mid-twelfth century the descendants and successors of the original warriors were becoming, to use the contemporary opprobrious term, "rustic," that is, less military, more peaceful and civilian, and their lands, originally granted for the support of a warrior group, became the endowment of a class of hereditary county administrators who, for many centuries, provided the sheriffs, the justices of the peace, and a large proportion of the members of the House of Commons.

One other aspect of the Norman Conquest[20] must now be discussed. It involved England in a long, if intermittent, struggle with France. Normandy, blocking the lower Seine, badly obstructed the Capetian kings in their efforts to establish their effective supremacy over the whole country. When Henry II added Anjou and his wife's inheritance of Aquitaine to the English territory, the problem was compounded, for the resulting Angevin empire covered a greater part of France than that controlled by the French king himself. The fates of England and France thus became so intertwined that, it has been said, the histories of the two countries during the Middle Ages can hardly be written separately. The conquest indeed left the French language, literature, art, and architecture predominant in the upper ranges of English society until well into the fourteenth century. And, as we shall see, as the French kings gradually increased their power, territorial involvement in France became an expensive curse for the English monarchy, as it became more and more engaged in a struggle with a country whose resources in money and manpower were much greater than its own.

[20] See pp. 104–05 for its economic effects.

CHAPTER FIVE

Henry II's foreign possessions far overshadowed the modest realm of England. King in England, feudal overlord of Wales, Scotland, and Ireland, in France his possessions far exceeded those of the French monarch himself.[1] Except for Brittany, he controlled France's Atlantic seaboard and the northern coast. One of his daughters married Henry the Lion, the powerful leader of the Welf party in Germany; another daughter married the king of Castile, and a third the Norman king of Sicily. Henry's power and reputation stood so high that in 1177 he was chosen as arbitrator in a dispute between the kings of Castile and Navarre. As one of the greatest international figures of the day, lord of vast possessions, he was able to give England only part of his attention. Because he was away from England for far longer periods than any of his predecessors, circumstances forced him to devise a system of government that could function in his absence. Although the various stages of the process are obscure, he was so successful that his son Richard I could spend all but five months of his ten-year reign away from the country.

---

[1] He possessed Normandy through his mother, Anjou, Maine, and Touraine through his father, Aquitaine from his wife.

Angevin Kingship and the Development of Government

Economic and Cultural Revival
Under Henry II

Henry reigned during an age of economic and cultural revival—an age of rising population and rising prices, when, in most parts of Europe, the area of land under the plow was greatly expanded and the towns grew in size and prosperity. The revival of education and letters generally known as the twelfth-century renaissance led to new speculation and developments in philosophy, theology, and literature. The Church, stimulated by the High Gregorian reform movement, had entered its most imaginative and constructive period, particularly in the development and definition of canon law. Such developments were most important during this epoch of English history when the greatest twelfth-century English lawyers were churchmen, for the results of their training in the more advanced and logical principles of canon law powerfully shaped the earliest and most constructive phase in the development of English common law.

Henry's court glittered with brilliant writers. William of Newburgh and Ralph de Diceto wrote their chronicles, and Giraldus Cambrensis gave the world a vivid autobiography. In his *Courtier's Trifles*, Walter Map depicted the mind and interests of a well-educated, well-connected churchman

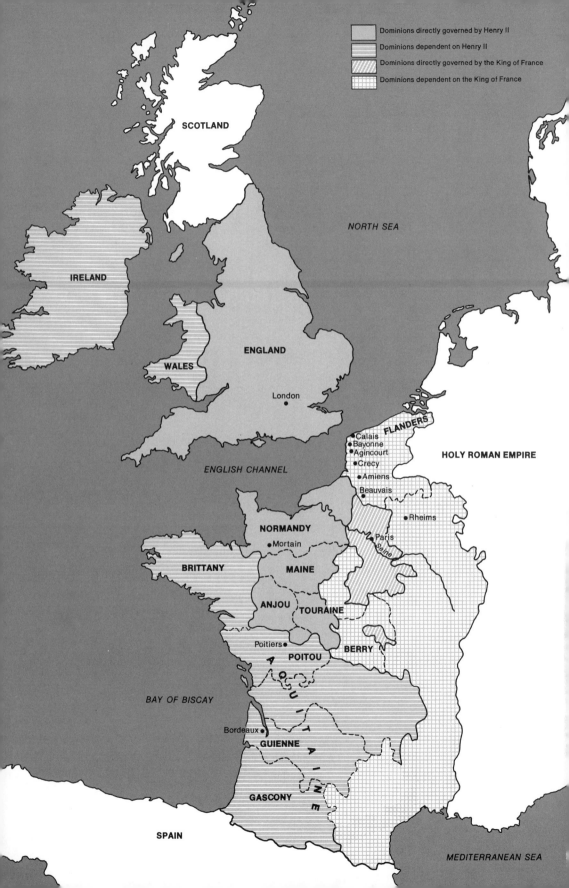

	Dominions directly governed by Henry II
	Dominions dependent on Henry II
	Dominions directly governed by the King of France
	Dominions dependent on the King of France

SCOTLAND

NORTH SEA

IRELAND

ENGLAND

WALES

London

HOLY ROMAN EMPIRE

ENGLISH CHANNEL

FLANDERS

Calais
Bayonne
Agincourt
Crecy
Amiens
Beauvais

Rheims

NORMANDY

Mortain

Paris

Seine

BRITTANY

MAINE

ANJOU

TOURAINE

BERRY

Poitiers

POITOU

A
Q
U
I
T
A
I
N
E

BAY OF BISCAY

Bordeaux

GUIENNE

GASCONY

SPAIN

MEDITERRANEAN SEA

Map of Medieval Angevin Empire.

who held a good position at the royal court. It is a strange compilation of rather weird fairy stories and tales (often highly scandalous) of some of the great figures of the day. One section half satirically enquired whether the royal court could validly be compared with hell. Civil servants wrote about their work: Ranulph Glanvill on the law; Richard FitzNeal, in the *Dialogue of the Exchequer,* giving the first extant description of any government department produced by one of its own members. John of Salisbury, a classical scholar who would have been distinguished in any age, wrote with considerable insight about problems of the state and political thought.

Henry II, himself a man of some learning, is said to have known all the languages spoken between the English Channel and the River Jordan. As a patron of art and letters he was generous; no less than twenty books dedicated to him are still extant. In other ways, also, Henry was well-fitted for his role in an age which demanded supreme vitality for successful kingship. He was a man of restless, relentless energy who could never be still. It was a matter for scandal that he could never sit patiently through the Mass. His court was perpetually on the move from one district to another: the courtiers and officials, weary, tired, and-jaded at the end of a day in the saddle, Henry fresh and fit for work. A man of fiery temper and uncontrolled passions and appetites, Henry was a mighty hunter of both animals and women: legend claimed that his hot-blooded family descended from a demon ancestress.

The Assize of Clarendon and the New Criminal Justice

Henry had a daunting task before him when he arrived in England in 1154. Although historians differ in their estimates of the devastations inflicted during Stephen's reign, it is clear that the restoration of more orderly and effective government was essential. First, Henry ordered the destruction of the "adulterine" castles—castles erected without royal permission during the previous reign. It is said that there were over 1,100 of these. Then he attempted to take back many of the royal demesnes which both Stephen and Matilda had granted away in return for aristocratic support.

The next, or perhaps simultaneous, task was the restoration of public order, the severely practical necessity of holding in check, even diminishing, the chronic violence which had grown far worse during the uncertainties of Stephen's reign. Henry could accomplish this only by establishing a wider control over the community. And he was quite as well aware as Henry I had been that such an extension of royal control could be very profitable. The problem became so onerous that its solution ultimately involved the development of new methods of judicial procedure in both criminal and civil matters. This massive governmental intervention in the life of the community produced beneficial results which endured for centuries, but at the time it was unfortunately tainted by an arbitrary element and by fiscal greed which provoked feudal discontent and, ultimately, under King John (1199–1216), led to feudal revolt and the issue of Magna Carta.

It used to be said that Henry II and his lawyers invented new legal procedures, but, although precedents were somewhat scattered and by no means complete, it seems more probable that they adopted and expanded methods which had already been used from time to time in the Anglo-Norman period, and even during Stephen's reign. But, although Henry II may not have been so inventive of legal forms and processes as historians once thought, he so extended these practices that he combined them into a new, progressive pattern of law. In both civil and criminal matters, new formulae appeared in the middle of the 1160s, but it is likely that a process of trial and error, now concealed from us, was going on all through the first decade of Henry's reign. The king's justices may well have been investigating cases all the time, and the king then, after various experiments had proved their worth, may have formulated definite rules for judicial proceedings. At most, we can advance no more than a plausible hypothesis on this point. The results, however, are clear enough. The king attempted to tighten up criminal justice, especially the means available for the detection of criminals, and to place quicker judicial remedies at the disposal of his subjects in one of the most important aspects of twelfth-century life, disputes concerning land.

In 1166 Henry issued the Assize of Clarendon which, among other things, established the basic form of criminal charge which lasted in English legal procedure until 1933. The relevant clause in the assize speaks for itself:

> The aforesaid King Henry by the counsel of all his barons, has ordained that, for the preservation of the peace and the enforcement of justice, inquiry shall be made in every shire and in every hundred through twelve of the more lawful men of the hundred and through four of the more lawful men of each vill [put] on oath to tell the truth, whether in their hundred or in their vill there is any man accused or publicly known as a robber or murderer or thief,[2] or anyone who has been a receiver of robbers or murderers or thieves, since the lord King has been King. And let the justices make this investigation in their presence and the sheriffs in their presence.

In effect, the clause set up in the shire a royal court under a royal justice, competent to hear indictments and to judge and punish offenders.

[2] Ten years later, forgery and arson were added to the list.

It thus seriously encroached upon the jurisdiction of the old customary courts and of the franchise courts.[3] Up to this time the accusation of offenders had been the responsibility of the injured party or his kindred: they had appealed (or called upon) the suspected man to answer their accusations. There were, however, long-standing precedents in various parts of the country for the collective accusation of offenders. Now, based upon these, the use of the jury drawn from the hundreds and the vills transferred the duty to the local community as a whole, and the institution of the grand jury became general and firmly based. On the king's orders, the countryside was drawn into an alliance with him for the suppression of wrongdoing, and the idea of crime as an offense against the community, a matter of public not merely private concern, became quite explicit.

Although it was a great advance, the benefits of this reform can easily be exaggerated. Henry had introduced a new method of accusation—only the first, if a vital stage—in criminal proceedings. There was no corresponding improvement in the method of trial. Trial itself still followed the traditional and irrational procedure of the ordeal. The Assize of Clarendon more or less tacitly admitted defeat at this point, by ordering that notorious characters who successfully passed the ordeal should, nevertheless, be banished from the realm. This admission that, in spite of improved methods of accusation, a criminal whose guilt was known to the whole countryside could clear himself by the established methods of trial, was obviously a confession of failure. In effect, the king invited the countryside to indulge in tale-bearing on a large scale, an excellent method of producing a long list of bad characters. The grand jury brought up rumors and suspicions as well as facts, but the facts were left for proof by antiquated, inadequate means.

An examination of the results from the Lincolnshire Assize Roll of 1202 amply confirms this pessimistic analysis. The crimes listed there were, in all probability, recent ones, for the royal justices had been in Lincolnshire in 1200 and 1201. Yet, there seem to have been the following cases: homicide, 114; robbery (often with violence), 89; wounding, 65; rape, 49; and a number of lesser crimes. The results were meager in the extreme: sixteen men who had fled and escaped capture were outlawed, eleven others had taken sanctuary in churches and were also outlawed, nine criminal churchmen were handed over to the ecclesiastical courts, and eight men were sent for trial by ordeal. Of these last, two were executed. Two executions and between twenty and thirty sentences of outlawry are hardly impressive as the total punishments inflicted after about 430 accusations of serious crime. Some improvement for trying the accused came in the early thirteenth century, when the petty jury gradually replaced the ordeal. Even

---

[3] An originally public court that the king had granted to a private individual, who then held its sessions and took the profits.

then, the apprehension and conviction of criminals remained a perennial problem. In the absence of any effective police force, the sanctions against crime remained appallingly weak, and at the end of the fifteenth century a Venetian ambassador noted with amazement the droves of criminals the country annually produced: "People are taken up every day by dozens, like birds in a covey, and especially in London; yet for all this they never cease to rob and murder in the streets."[4]

Reforms in Civil Justice: The Birth of English Common Law

In matters of civil justice, Henry II's reforms were much more successful. He developed the use of royal writs for private litigation; he put the inquest, or jury system, at the disposal of his subjects in cases dealing with land; and he established as a working principle of law the defense, against violent eviction, of the man in possession of land—"the beatitude of seisin,"[5] as the great historian Maitland called it.

Many men had been wrongfully dispossessed of their lands under Stephen, or the opposing factions had then made different and conflicting grants of the same estates. Until this time, all except tenants-in-chief and particularly favored men could obtain settlement of such disputes only in the honorial courts. Now the king allowed men to bring cases into his court, if they so wished, to determine rights of possession. To do so became most attractive to litigants, because this court was flexible and could offer procedures swifter and more rational than the traditional methods of the honorial courts.

First, the king placed at the disposal of freemen, who could afford to buy them, writs ordering cases concerning the possession of land to be held in a royal court. Writs might also be obtained in other circumstances ordering unwilling lords to do justice in their own courts, and it was ultimately established that no man need appear in any court to answer for his estates except upon a royal writ. Second, the king made the inquest, or the jury system, available to private individuals. Since the Norman Conquest, possibly before, the Crown had possessed, and had from time to time used, a method of ascertaining facts more rational than the older processes of trial and judgment practiced in the honorial courts, the barbarous process of the judicial duel, or trial by battle. This other method was the inquest of sworn recognition by which a group of local people, or a jury, swore upon oath from their own knowledge to the facts posed by particular questions. Henry now allowed the use of this process in certain types of cases, particularly

---

[4] *A Relation, or Rather a True Account of the Island of England,* ed. C. A. Sheyd (Camden Society, London, 1847), p. 36.
[5] "Seisin," that is, possession.

those involving dispossession from estates. These possessory, or petty, assizes,[6] as they came to be called, were intended both to secure freeholders in their property by more expeditious and more rational processes and to reduce self-help and, therefore, disorder, by giving temporary settlements in disputes about estates. They decided upon recent facts of possession but left untouched the ultimate rights of ownership, which could be settled by a longer and more elaborate form of lawsuit called a Grand Assize. In fact, however, the verdicts of the petty assizes generally came to be accepted as permanent settlements.

Henry's judicial innovations were completed by his system of itinerant justices and his court of Common Pleas. The itinerant justices can again be traced back, with some differences, to practices under William II and Henry I, but, once again, it was Henry II who turned an occasional expedient into a regular institution. These traveling justices could deal with any matter brought before them, and their work soon proved to be so extensive that Henry divided the country into a number[7] of judicial circuits that were frequently changed, probably according to the legal staff available to man them. In 1166 there were two circuits, and by 1173 the number had increased to six.

By about 1178 the court of Common Pleas had also come into existence as the result of a number of obscure experiments: some of the justices now remained permanently with the king to hear cases. As Henry II was perpetually on the move, the court perpetually moved with him, which could cause immense inconvenience and expense to litigants. One of them, Richard of Anstey, set down his experiences.[8] After long preliminary hearings in the ecclesiastical courts to decide on the validity of a marriage, Richard took his case about the family estates to the royal court. He followed the king to Romsey, from Romsey to Windsor, then to London, back to Windsor, on to Reading and Wallingford, back again to London, and finally to Woodstock. Besides other expenses, mainly in the ecclesiastical courts, these exasperating journeys cost him £25.7.0, plus a present of £24 to the king's doctor, 100 marks to the king, and one gold mark[9] to the queen. To meet his costs, he had to borrow £95 from Jewish usurers, much of it at the appalling interest rate of 87 percent a year.[10] Though the means

---

[6] *Novel disseisin* decided cases of recent dispossession of land; *mort d'ancestor* protected an heir who had been kept out of his heritage; *darrein presentment* protected rights of patronage in churches; *Utrum* decided whether a property belonged to the Church in "free alms" (i.e., free of feudal services) or by lay fee and, therefore, whether jurisdiction lay with an ecclesiastical or a secular court.

[7] They were not stabilized until the early fourteenth century.

[8] His journey dates from 1163, but the same kind of thing could easily have happened after the establishment of the court of Common Pleas as long as it journeyed with King Henry.

[9] A mark was 13/4; a gold mark, £6.

[10] The magnitude of these sums can be realized from the fact that a contemporary landowner was considered very prosperous if he had an income of £20 a year.

of justice were improving, they remained inconvenient and expensive. It must have been a great relief to litigants when by about 1178, the court came to be more or less fixed at Westminster—although even then it moved from time to time.

All the judicial improvements were initially matters of legal process, more certain, more rational procedures in litigation. At first the royal justices merely applied more uniform rules of procedure to the existing law as they found it in their movements from district to district. As time went on, however, they came to affect the substantial content of the law itself. A more uniform content thus, in time, replaced the variations of the ancient regional codes—and so the English "common law" was born. This term means no more than law common to the whole country, though its application was never complete in medieval times.[11]

Historians once claimed that Henry II, through these new judicial procedures, made a direct, premeditated attack upon the powers of the magnates and that his reforms were, therefore, highly unpopular with the feudal lords. Any such theory was certainly based upon inadequate information about twelfth-century social and political developments. All public authority, all social restraints were at that time so weak that no king could possibly even consider endangering them by deliberately taking away powers from great men upon whose cooperation the peace and good order of the countryside in the last resort depended. The development of the possessory assizes was stimulated by the vast amount of litigation over land, the result of violent dispossessions during Stephen's reign. Although this development deprived the honorial courts of litigation, it seems that it met acute needs already present in a changing feudal world.

Social and economic changes were enfeebling the feudal communities, the honours, as coherent and workable units. From their early days, subinfeudation had become more and more extensive, even to the point where the knight's fees were split into fractions. This subdivision produced military and civil consequences fatal to the cohesion of the original, fairly simple, feudal organization. When tenants held halves, quarters, and even smaller fractions of knight's fees, it became difficult for the lord, and tenant-in-chief, to raise flesh-and-blood knights for service from them. A subtenant would claim that he could not be expected to serve with the feudal levy in person as he did not possess the full amount of land. The lord, in such circumstances, often took a monetary payment in lieu of service. So, to some extent, the honour got out of control. It lost its coherence as a working military community.

Moreover, the lords' positions within the honours grew confused in other ways. The possessions of the English tenants-in-chief were not great

---

[11] Kent retained its own peculiar system of inheritance known as "gavel-kind," that is, the division of the inheritance among the sons instead of complete inheritance by the eldest son.

compact blocks of territory like those of the great continental barons. Their lands were widely scattered, much interspersed with those of others, so that one lord's tenants were always in intimate contact with those of other, different lords. With increasing sales of land and marriages and inheritances between families which belonged to different honours, the original simple formula (if it ever existed) of one man as the tenant of one, and only one, honour disappeared. Men came to hold estates within several honours. Which of several lords then had the right of jurisdiction over them? Moreover, what would happen if and when a tenant of one honour brought a plea in land against a tenant of another? In whose court was the plea to be heard? As early as the reign of Henry I, it had been laid down "if it is between the vassals of two lords let it be tried in the county [court]"—thus ignoring both lords and their honorial courts.

The honorial courts became less competent as the feudal structure became more complex. The king was stepping in to fill the gaps in the feudal community. In doing so, particularly through the itinerant justices, he was also increasing control of the central government over the localities by increasing contact with all free men, not merely with the baronial classes: a contact very much strengthened by the fact that the new justice was very popular with minor landowners. In the Danelaw, enormous numbers of people profited from the tours of the itinerant justices by going to law about very small parcels of land. Apart from comparatively minor procedural points which they attacked, the feudal classes came to regard Henry's judicial innovations as essential. The great feudal magnates of 1215, who dominated the discussions which produced Magna Carta, demanded that the possessory assizes should be held in each county four times a year—too frequent a service, in fact, for the government to provide.

Royal Finances

Henry II's reforms were by no means limited to judicial matters. Throughout his reign and those of his sons, Richard I (1189–99) and John (1199–1216), experiments in administrative reorganization were almost continuous. Although this increasing governmental activity made a most impressive contribution to the development of English institutions, it was also, unfortunately, tinged with harsh fiscality and arbitrary royal action which provoked increasing, and often justified, resentment. This resentment reached a bursting point in the feudal revolt which, in 1215, led to the issue of Magna Carta. King John's unpleasant personality and his more extreme methods provoked to action a baronage already resentful of the whole trend of Angevin government from 1154 onward. It is hardly possible to overstress the importance of the royal finances as a stimulant of medieval English developments. Henry II was unfortunate in coming to a monarchy the resources of which had been seriously depleted. William the Conqueror's successors, for political reasons, had granted away much of his extensive royal demesne. Henry I's revenues, by dint of much extortion, had reached about £25–30,000 a year. During the first five years of his reign, Henry II's English income had shrunk to about £10,000, though, as far as figures went, in the end he raised his income to the old level and, in some years, pressed it even higher.

Nevertheless, a long-term deterioration in the financial position of the Crown occurred, a deterioration due to both military and economic causes. Henry II waged war in France for long periods, but, unfortunately for his coffers, the feudal host was an instrument suitable only for the defense of the territory in which its knights held their lands. The period of service which could be demanded from the feudal host was short. Although it had originally been undefined, feudal opinion, by this time, had restricted it to forty days a year, a time span obviously useless for service abroad: If contrary winds held up the transport fleet, the period of service might well be over before the army even set foot on its campaign territory. Though Henry took "scutages," or money payments in lieu of services, the feudal army gradually fell to pieces. From 1166 to 1197 there had been no general summons of the feudal host for service abroad. When at last Richard I finally called it out in the latter year, the Bishop of Lincoln tried to claim that it could not be made to serve out of the country. Henry II, therefore, could not wage war abroad without paying considerable numbers of professional mercenaries. This was an extremely serious matter, for the twelfth century was a period of inflation during which the wages of mercenary knights rose by 300 percent.

Henry II made various attempts to increase his revenues. At the beginning of his reign he resumed Crown lands, but later, for political reasons, like his predecessors, he again made extensive grants from them. He took scutages from his tenants-in-chief, but he lost control of the geld: its yield had seriously declined, and he made no attempt to levy it after 1174. He imposed additional sums, or increments, on the county farms,[12] for example, £10 on the county farm of Buckinghamshire. By the end of the reign such piecemeal additions had improved the country's revenues by about 10 percent, but Henry made no systematic effort to reassess the farms at their true value in an age of rising prices. Another method of raising money was by "amercements," or fines, a method made more profitable by the expansion of the judicial circuits, or the Eyre.[13] Amercements could be heavy: the pleas of the Forest in Hampshire alone brought in over £2,000 in the 1170s. Once again, the profits of justice were highly unpopular.

Henry II also tried to obtain more money from feudal sources. In 1166,

---

[12] The sum that the sheriff was expected to raise annually from each county.
[13] See pp. 90–91.

more from financial than military motives, he carried out an overhaul of the feudal system. As we have already seen, kings, up to this time, had not directly concerned themselves with subinfeudation. Henry already knew the amount of service due from each barony to the Crown. He now enquired from his tenants-in-chief how many knights they had enfeoffed before the death of Henry I, how many they had enfeoffed since that time, and how many were left chargeable on the demesne. With the information supplied by this enquiry, Henry tried to obtain an advantage both ways. If too few knights had been enfeoffed to perform the entire service, the fief was assessed for scutage on the numbers of the original quota: if the number of knights enfeoffed exceeded the quota, the quota was correspondingly increased. The results were not entirely successful, for the barons, not unnaturally, resisted these new demands. In the end, Henry was forced to compromise: the barons paid only on their enfeoffments to the death of Henry I, not on those made under Stephen.

The magnates, although recalcitrant, probably did not resent such action nearly as much as they did Henry's arbitrary dealings in matters of inheritance and justice. He undoubtedly manipulated the vagueness of feudal conventions very much to his own advantage in such matters; for example, taking excessive reliefs before allowing heirs to succeed to their fathers' estates. Moreover, in spite of the new legal procedures, royal justice was far from impartial. As in Iron Curtain and some underdeveloped countries today, justice was intermingled with political patronage and used as a means of exercising tight control over men's social and political activities. As Richard FitzNeal, Henry's treasurer, wrote:

> To some he [the King] does full justice for nothing, in consideration of their past services or mere goodness of heart; but to others (and it is only human nature) he will not give way either for love or money; sometimes owing to the deserts of those who hold what is sought, sometimes because the petitioners have done nothing to deserve it, being censured for offending against the realm or the king himself.[14]

Henry, for political reasons, showed excessive favor to some men in matters of justice; others he made aware of his displeasure by heavy amercements, fines, or even the confiscation of property. Once Henry even deprived a landowner of his estate for refusing to give dinner to one of the royal huntsmen.

Local Government and the General Eyres

In 1170 Henry returned to England after an absence of four years. However, while he was still abroad, numerous complaints had reached him

[14] *Dialogus de Scaccario: The Course of the Exchequer*, ed. and trans. C. Johnson (London, 1950), p. 120.

about the wrongdoing and corruption of those responsible for local government. On his return he, therefore, divided the country into circuits and appointed commissioners for each, providing them with a long list of questions to be answered in detail by representatives of the shires and the hundreds. This enquiry is misleadingly known as the Inquest of Sheriffs; it was, in fact, a general inquest into the state of the country, into the behavior of all officials, whether royal or baronial, into the wrongful leakage of revenue, and into the condition of the royal manors. The enquiry was so comprehensive that one historian has compared it with Domesday Book, but, unfortunately, unlike Domesday, only a few fragments of the returns have survived. But its result was noteworthy: most of the sheriffs who had been in office since the beginning of the reign and who, since 1135, had again been feudal magnates, were dismissed from office. This dismissal finally marked the end of the great feudal sheriffs. Henry replaced them mostly by officials trained in the Exchequer, less closely connected with the counties by property and, like Henry I's official sheriffs, more amenable to royal influence, as well as being more skilled administrators.

One of the main difficulties of medieval monarchs was to keep administration, especially local administration, free from its perpetual tendency to corruption. No public morality as we understand it had yet arisen, or was to arise for many centuries. Those in office expected to feather their own nests, and all men recognized that public service was the quickest way to make a fortune. Ralph of Diceto claimed that Henry II tried by turns all classes of men in his efforts to find honest justices, but all failed him. Constant vigilance was essential to keep such gains within conventionally decent limits. The Inquest of Sheriffs probably set the precedent for recurrent inquests in the shires and hundreds about the king's affairs and about all local affairs, inquests which came to be known as General Eyres. In 1170 the commissioners had reported to the king, who acted upon their reports. The justices in Eyre, however, were empowered to take action themselves upon the wrongs which their enquiries brought to light in their circuits through the countryside.

The first surviving list of instructions for the General Eyre dates from 1194, but it had been going on long before, and this first list has much in common with that of 1170. The articles of the Eyre were wide in scope, covering crime, common pleas in land (the possessory assizes and so on), the king's financial interests, his rights in escheated lands and ecclesiastical patronage, the tallage (or taxation) of royal cities and demesnes. The Eyre could, in fact, cover anything the king wished. At first the king may have planned to hold an annual Eyre, but by Henry III's time (1216–72) they took place only every three or four years. As time went on the enquiry became more and more elaborate, it took longer to conduct, and it became more and more unpopular. Although men welcomed its activity in hearing the civil pleas of the shire and its repression of corruption, they detested its use as a means of raising money. It generally cost the community a great deal in fines and amercements for many small offenses, often merely of a technical nature. So oppressive did the visits of the justices become in the eyes of the population that, it is said, the inhabitants of Cornwall, in 1233, hearing there was to be a General Eyre, fled to the woods en masse rather than face it. By 1258 people looked upon it as a necessity tinged by abuses, and Henry III was made to promise that it would not be inflicted upon the country more than once in seven years. From then onward, Eyres took place at longer and longer intervals, until at the end of the thirteenth century their work was divided among a number of more specialized commissions.

Relations with the Church

Henry II early turned his attention to the Church, but here his designs were frustrated. There were two main points at issue: the powers of the papacy over the English clergy and the problem of criminous clerks, or privilege of clergy. William the Conqueror, although extremely devout, had been determined to maintain complete control of the Church in England. His two sons followed the same policy. In so doing, they set themselves in opposition to a powerful papal reform movement determined that, to avoid corruption, the Church must emancipate itself from lay control and make itself the sole judge of the affairs and the conduct of the clergy. Stephen in his weakness had allowed churchmen to take appeals to the papal curia, thus weakening the traditional stand of the Crown against such practices. On the second point, clerics accused of crime claimed exemption from royal jurisdiction and the right to be tried exclusively in the bishops' courts.

In 1164, in the constitutions of Clarendon, Henry II declared that in future no judicial appeals were to be made to Rome; that no ecclesiastic was to leave the country without the king's consent; that bishops and abbots were to do homage to the king before their consecration, thus emphasizing their position as royal vassals; and that clerks convicted in ecclesiastical courts should no longer be protected from further punishment by the king.

Henry's exchancellor, Thomas Becket, now Archbishop of Canterbury, denounced these constitutions out-of-hand much to the embarrassment of many of the higher clergy and even of Pope Alexander III himself, for Becket's extreme claims for the complete exemption of clerks from secular justice had not yet been anywhere established. Henry was a man of fierce temper; Becket intransigent, theatrical, and petty. The clash of these two violent temperaments made compromise almost impossible. Becket went into exile, and after negotiations lasting on and off for six years returned to England, only to be murdered in his own cathedral by four of Henry's over-zealous knights. This tragedy forced the king to give way. Henry, after doing abject penance, yielded the principle of appeals to Rome, with the reservation that they must not result in harm to his Crown or his kingdom, and he allowed the Church full jurisdiction over its criminal members. Punishments in the ecclesiastical courts were much lighter than those in the secular courts—and in the future no clerk could be hanged for murder or theft if it was his first offense.

Lasting Influences of Henry II's Reign

Thus, from the middle of the twelfth century, we can see very important changes taking place. Most significantly, the feudal community of the honours was declining, less as a result of royal policy, although this certainly assisted the process, but far more as the consequence of its own inherent inability to cope with the new patterns and needs of a changing world. The corollary to the decline of the honour and the feudal community was the strengthening of the public community, the shire, in alliance with, almost at the command of, the king.

Since the Norman Conquest the shire had, perhaps, been losing some of its power as a public community. It had, of course, retained its old powers of customary jurisdiction. For a long time, however, it obtained no new functions, while immunities and franchises[15] encroached on many of its old ones. The view of frankpledge was a common franchise, and it excluded the royal officer, the sheriff, from his regular supervision of the hundred. Some feudal lords had been granted the right of serving the king's writs, and the sheriff was not permitted even to enter their lands. Now, as the result of the royal initiative and the royal reforms in legal procedure, the shire filled the gap left by the decline of the feudal community and at the same time acquired new powers. By allowing new scope to the judicial and supervisory powers of the central government, the shire changed its character. Before the Norman Conquest, on the whole, it had been a small self-governing community, receiving very few orders from the central government. In the twelfth century it owed its growing part in the life of the community less to this semi-independent position, more to the new tasks which the king chose that it should perform. Although it was no longer so powerful as a local self-regulating community, it grew more important as it received direction and orders from Westminster. The justices coming to the shire under the Assize of Clarendon, for example, came to carry out the king's orders, and no lands whatsoever were immune from their jurisdiction. They dealt with the entire county and could enter any of the liberties, even the greatest.

This tendency to make use of the shire became even more prominent

---

[15] A franchise was a regalian right that had passed into private hands, as, for example, when the right to hold a hundred court was given to a private landowner.

as time went on. In 1197 it became a unit for taxation. In 1205 King John established a hierarchy of constables within it for the better keeping of the peace. That it became the unit of general administration as the government took unto itself more and more functions was due not to any inherent natural development but to the fact that the Crown used it and gave it new duties. In so doing, the Crown also brought into being a new class of administrators. With the final fall of the baronial sheriff after the inquest of 1170, the magnates, to some extent, withdrew from the shire court, and the onerous burden of the new duties fell on the knights, a body of men already experienced in justice and administration through their work in the honorial courts and more inclined to civilian duties as they were called on less and less for military service. The fortunate accident that magnates' estates in England were scattered over many counties, instead of being concentrated in great compact blocks of territory, made it impossible for any magnate to dominate a shire completely. This ancient unit of administration could therefore be developed for new public duties.

This extension and redevelopment of its functions strengthened the shire as the focus of a kind of local patriotism. For most people, it had always been their *patria*, a homeland for which they had a profound emotional sentiment far more vivid than that which they felt for the country as a whole. By the end of the twelfth century knights resented interference by strangers from outside this small community. By the mid-fifteenth century, if not earlier, they felt that the community's own landowners, and no others, should represent it in Parliament. Even in the great civil war of the seventeenth century, many families took sides between king and Parliament on local, or county, rather than on national issues.

Henry's expedients which in the long run so profoundly affected English life were more successful than his immediate policies. In spite of his arbitrary manipulations of feudalism, he failed to reorganize his financial system to gain what should have been the monarchy's fair increment from rising prosperity and rising prices. If there was reform in the financial system, it was more or less confined to technical details in accounting procedures at the Exchequer. Though the sessions of the Exchequer could be held anywhere, after 1156 its usual meeting place was at Westminster, and it was settling down to a steady grinding routine. Even so, although it was a very powerful department by comparison with anything which had gone before, it was, by modern standards, inefficient. Many of its payments were almost permanently in arrears; it sometimes took years to obtain the moneys due from the sheriffs. It was far from unknown for the Exchequer to be claiming arrears from the heirs of a sheriff long after his period of office and long after his death.

In spite of all his efforts, Henry's continental commitments in the end exceeded his resources. He died unsuccessfully defending Berry and Maine against the resurgent French monarchy; dying in utter defeat,

murmuring in anguish and delirium, "Shame, shame on a conquered king."
His sons found the defense of their French possessions even more difficult,
and finally the strains of this task produced violent reaction under King
John.

Institutional Changes Under King John

King John continued to advance the vast institutional changes of twelfth-
century England, those changes which monarchs imposed by their dynamic
will over the comparative inertia of a society based upon immemorial custom. Once again, we see a marked advance in the process of putting government on a written basis. Under Henry II the practice had developed of
keeping duplicate copies of certain writs and instructions at Westminster.
By the end of the century more methodical ways were everywhere developing. The papal registers, although they go back in some form or another to
the fourth century, began to be systematically kept in 1198, the first year
of Pope Innocent III's reign (1198–1216). The French governmental registers
appeared at the same time. In England, in addition to the long-existent
Pipe Rolls, the Exchequer instituted its Receipt Rolls in the early 1160s, to
be followed by the Memoranda Rolls under King John. For legal matters,
the earliest surviving Curia Regis Rolls date from 1194, the Assize Rolls
from a few years later.[16] In the early years of John's reign, the Chancery,
probably inspired by Hubert Walter, followed the example of the Exchequer
and the courts: the Charter Rolls, the Patent Rolls, the Close Rolls, the
Fine, Liberate, and Norman Rolls[17] all appeared between 1199 and 1205.
From then onward, the government had a much more exact record of all
its transactions and concessions. Richard I and John also intensified
financial pressure with new experiments in taxation on land and movable
property and a short-lived experiment with a customs system (1203–05).

To do all this, the government had to increase the number of its
officials. It was no longer possible, even in theory, to govern the country
through a few officials, drawn from members of the magnate class, who

[16] The date when the first rolls were compiled is unknown, but most probably it was
some time in the reign of Henry II.
[17] Assize Rolls—records of cases heard before the justices of Assize.
Charter Rolls—copies of royal grants made to subjects.
Patent Rolls—copies of royal letters patent, open letters, conveying royal grants and
    orders.
Close Rolls—copies of letters close, closed and sealed letters, of a less public nature
    than letters patent and generally addressed to individuals.
Fine Rolls—records of sums of money or valuable objects offered to the king for the
    grant of estates, privileges, enjoyment of the royal favor, and so on.
Liberate Rolls—records of precepts sent from the Chancery to the Exchequer ordering
    payments of various kinds.
Norman Rolls—records of business concerning the duchy of Normandy while it was
    the possession of the English Crown.

were in the king's confidence and sufficiently interested to devote themselves to administration. A new problem was arising, and towards the end
of the century it became acute: a problem essentially that of the extended
executive work of government and the relationship of the new bureaucracy
to the people with whom it came into contact. The combination of greater
interference, the possibilities opened up by greater precision, and the
dubious personal activities of some of the new civil servants, especially of
the numerous Poitevins whom John employed, was enough to produce
considerable discontent. By the first decade of the thirteenth century, after
fifty years of development, the king's feudal tenants found that the Angevin
system of government needed adjustment and revision.

A potentially explosive situation was made infinitely worse by the
personality of King John and by the state of affairs in the Angevin possessions in France. John was a man of ferocious, at times almost demented,
energy. But, unfortunately, there were times when he sank into strange
fits of inertia and lassitude, when he allowed grandiose plans to fall apart
from lack of attention. The results of this were more important abroad,
however, than in his domestic policy.

As noted earlier, Henry II had found increasing difficulty in holding
his own abroad against the resurgent French monarchy. In fact, he died in
the midst of defeat. Richard I spent the first part of his reign on the Third
Crusade, the later part continuing the struggle against Philip Augustus of
France. The struggle grew more and more unequal. Philip Augustus drove
John out of Normandy in 1204, and John spent the next few years
organizing a series of expensive alliances to take his revenge and win
back the duchy. These schemes were finally ruined by the French defeat
of an Anglo-Flemish-German army at Bouvines in 1214 and John's own
simultaneous failure against another French army in Poitou and Anjou.
Many of the greater English families possessed ancestral estates in
Normandy, and although they had supported his war plans only in the
most grudging way, they now laid the blame for their Norman losses at his
door. He had lost prestige by failing in war, the most disastrous and final
way in which a medieval king could lose reputation and bring upon himself
the anger and contempt of his vassals.

The Revolt of the Barons:
Magna Carta

From 1204 onward, tensions grew ever stronger, until at last in 1214 part
of the baronage revolted. This event and its results should not be considered a constitutional crisis of a modern kind about matters of high
government policy: the question at issue was not one of despotism versus
liberty in modern terms—which, indeed, men would hardly have understood at all in 1214. The barons were in no way attempting to regain a lost

control over royal policy. On really important matters affecting the policy of the kingdom, John did not cease to go on taking the counsel of his barons as his ancestors had done. In this he had no choice, for no enterprise of any moment could hope to succeed except as a cooperative effort between king and barons. During the first half of his reign, at least the greater barons and ecclesiastics frequently met the king in council. Indeed, it is from John's reign that the first writ of summons to a bishop to attend the royal council survives, and in 1213 the king ordered the attendance of four discreet men from every shire at a council. The concessions which the king ultimately made in Magna Carta never mentioned the question of consent to policy, only consent to financial exactions.

Autocracy existed only in the executive sphere. It was, in the end, the combination of financial exaction and arbitrary "justice"—the invasion of property rights through the exercise of the king's arbitrary will as a means of political-*cum*-financial coercion, taken to greater lengths than Henry II had taken them—that provoked revolt. The methods required to carry on over-ambitious war policies finally brought nemesis on a monarchy financially inadequately equipped to support them.

Richard I's financial exactions had been heavy. In addition to his taxes on land and movables, his ministers had raised a feudal aid to pay his ransom.[18] He had sold sheriffdoms to the highest bidder, thus encouraging extortion on the part of officials. He had sold numerous concessions, such as borough charters. So great was his need for money that he is said to have remarked that he would sell London itself if he could find a bidder. John's voracity was no less demanding. In addition to an experimental customs system, he raised the county farms,[19] and the details of the sheriffs' receipts and expenditure were more carefully checked. He evidently tried to turn scutage into a general tax, for he levied no less than eleven scutages in fifteen years. Even Henry II had levied only eight in his entire reign of thirty-five years, some of them at rates of only a third of his son's levies. In 1212, John ordered another enquiry into the fiefs. Although in the troubles that followed nothing came of this enquiry, men feared that it was the harbinger of great demands. In the end, it was the imposition of a very heavy scutage in 1214 that provided an immediate occasion for revolt.

Activity in the royal household more than paralleled activity in the new formalized great government departments. When he was in England, John perpetually moved about the countryside, supervising the localities. To meet the urgent need of money for war, he arranged for its quicker collection by bypassing the Exchequer—putting control of much of the revenue under his chamber, which, being part of the royal household, was,

---

[18] Richard was captured near Vienna in 1192 on his way home from Palestine and held for ransom by the Emperor Henry VI for 150,000 marks.
[19] A fixed payment made for holding an office or an estate for a specified period.

unlike the Exchequer, always with the king—and by establishing provincial treasuries in certain royal castles. He also kept the supervision of local government as far as possible in the hands of a very narrow group of people, many of them Poitevins, closely allied to the personnel of the household: men who, though devoted to the king, certainly abused their powers and positions in his interests—and in their own.

Above all, John practiced that peculiar form of "justice" (for want of a better term) that had been so characteristic of his father, Henry II. At the same time, in his hands, it became more active and possibly more extreme. Although it has been plausibly argued that through his judicial activities John was a good king to most of his subjects and that he was popular in the countryside and in the towns, he was a most arbitrary feudal overlord. For example, he forced John of Chester to pay a fine of 7,000 marks before receiving his barony; he forced William de Braose to pay 5,000 marks before receiving his Irish lands, both quite excessive sums. De Braose's fine completely ruined him. The king sold wardships[20] at prices which could hardly be recovered by fair means during a minority, and he disparaged feudal widows by forcing them to marry his allegedly low-born foreign servants.

The charter, while accepting the institutional developments of the Angevins, for the first time introduced stability into these feudal relationships. Henry II's legal innovations had indeed become so popular that, while demanding some comparatively minor adjustments, the barons also asked for their extension. Clause 18 stated that the possessory assizes should be held in each county four times a year—a demand so far beyond the capacity of the government to fulfill that later reissues limited these circuits to one a year. The new stability introduced into the feudal relationship was very much to the advantage of the baronial classes: It limited the relief for a barony to £100, that for a knight's fee to 100 shillings—what the barons conveniently, but untruthfully, claimed to be ancient custom! Thus, by completely divorcing reliefs from the capital value of the fees in question, the charter protected the tenant and closed a valuable means of discipline and a valuable source of revenue to the king. He could no longer indicate his favor or his displeasure by arbitrarily varying the relief, and it was no longer possible periodically to take his share from the growing wealth of baronial and knightly estates. Moreover, in the future no more than a reasonable profit, without waste of stock and chattels, was to be taken from land under wardship, and such estates were to be returned to the heir in good condition when he came of age. Widows were not to be compelled to marry. The three customary aids which the king could take

---

[20] When a tenant-in-chief died leaving a child as his heir, it was quite usual for the king to sell or freely grant the guardianship of the child (until the age of his majority) and control of the lands to third parties.

without consent were to be levied at reasonable rates; all other aids and scutage, only after consent had been obtained. In all such matters, the tenants-in-chief were to treat their own tenants as the king treated them.

These matters concerned the feudal classes alone. They were naturally most concerned, because at all these points King John, his father, and his brother, all out for what financial profits they could get, had seriously abused the feudal relationship. In the main, Magna Carta was a feudal document in a feudal setting, but it was a feudal document with something of a difference. It was one of many such charters issued in various European countries during the twelfth, thirteenth, and early fourteenth centuries, but, almost alone among them, it extended protection to the feudal sub-tenants and to all free men in general—partly, no doubt, because tenurial relationships in England had already become so complicated that many tenants-in-chief held part of their lands as the subtenants of others. There were few rigid distinctions within the feudal hierarchy. It was, therefore, often to the material advantage, even of magnates, that lesser men should share their privileges. Some clauses in Magna Carta protected the Crown's debtors; others protected townsmen and even the livelihood of villeins. The famous Clause 39 in theory granted impartial methods of judicial procedure to all free men, though these were, in 1215, only a minority of the population.

The revolt of 1214 has often been described as the first great constitutional crisis in English history and Magna Carta as the country's first great constitutional document. This misconception was originally due to an anachronistic interpretation of the charter's background and of some of its individual clauses by fourteenth-century lawyers: interpretations later, in their turn, taken up and greatly extended by seventeenth-century lawyers in their arguments with the early Stuart kings on constitutional points.[21] If the charter is correctly interpreted, however, no constitutional theory whatsoever can be found there. It was not until about 1244 that a new generation of barons, dissatisfied with both royal political policies and the royal conduct of affairs, began to think in terms of taking over the executive and running the administration and the country in the king's name. There was no sign of any such constitutional program in 1215. It will be obvious from the detailed points already made that Magna Carta was not a written constitution; it was, above all, a document of *legal* definitions, concerned with very practical, businesslike points of the relationship between the king and his subjects and between different categories of subjects at points where they had been seriously abused. It substituted defini-

[21] In the fourteenth century the term "lawful judgment of peers" was interpreted to mean "trial by jury," a process that existed only in embryo in 1215. With the decline of villeinage, the term "no free man" came to be interpreted as "no man of whatever estate or condition he may be." These interpretations extended what had originally been the privileges of a group to the whole community.

tion for vagueness in the feudal relationship and thus restricted the arbitrary tendencies which had been so strong in Angevin government. It was not a charter of liberty, but of liberties. The abstract sense of this word did not appear in the English language until the end of the fifteenth century. Society was still too violent for an abstraction like liberty to have had much practical effect: a *liberty*, at this time, meant a special right or privilege, a franchise, an exemption to one's own advantage. Selfish as such privileges now seem, they were then the most secure defense against arbitrary government.

The sanctions which the barons imposed for the maintenance of the charter fully reveal its nature and its limitations. Clause 61 appointed a committee of twenty-five to oversee its execution. These twenty-five in no way formed a cabinet. They were to keep watch over the king's actions, to see that he dealt fairly with applications for the redress of individual grievances under the terms of the charter, and if he refused "they (the twenty-five), together with the community of the entire country, shall distress and injure us in all ways possible, namely by capturing our castles, lands and possessions in all ways that they can—until they secure redress according to their own decision, saving our person and the person of our queen and the persons of our children." Such action was hardly a political procedure in the normal sense of the term: it was an extension of the legal process of distraint, distraint upon the royal property.

One must admit that a sanction of this kind was crude in the extreme. Yet, after all, Magna Carta was the first notable attempt at opposition and control of the king, and first attempts to deal with any problem are generally somewhat crude. Although churchmen had developed sophisticated political theories, that even the lay magnates, illiterate as they were, could perhaps discuss intelligently, theories, at that time, outran practice. Faced with the problem of controlling a developed executive, men had little previous experience to draw upon. The crisis of 1215 was the first major stage of the baronial apprenticeship in opposition, and one might, therefore, expect their methods to lack finesse.

Magna Carta legally restricted the king's actions at points where they had been most oppressive to his subjects. In so doing, it powerfully affected future developments, for it closed valuable sources of revenue and kept the monarchy poor. Although reissues of the charter, among other controversial provisions, omitted a clause (no. 25) that the county farms should never be raised, the reduction of income under Henry III was quite considerable. It meant that in future the monarchy would have to rely much more upon the consent of its subjects to increase its income. For a century money was to be granted in return for confirmations of the charter, and the principle of consent to aids ultimately became the basis of consent to all taxation. The monarchy had lost one of the main foundations of arbitrary power.

CHAPTER SIX

Pioneer economic historians in the nineteenth century gave their readers a fairly simple picture of medieval agrarian organization: the picture of the manor. Their conclusions were justified on the limited evidence then available, but more extensive modern research has shown that their definitions have only a limited value. Nevertheless, the easiest way to understand rural conditions in the Middle Ages is to take their picture as a comparative model noting against it the many regional variations which existed even in a country as small as England.

According to the classic model, by the eleventh century the village and the manor had developed together in midland and southern England. The houses of the peasantry and laborers, with little yards around them, lay on either side of a village street, for as yet there were no farm houses scattered in the midst of the fields. The fields themselves, either two or three, with one left fallow every year,[1] were vast open fields divided into furlong strips, alloted to the different cultivators, each strip along its length distinguished by hazel rods or other rough-and-ready landmarks, with turf

---

[1] In the mid-thirteenth century, villages were about evenly divided between two- and three-field systems. Most historians argue that there was a gradual switch from two fields to three and view this as progressive in that more land could be cropped annually. It is arguable, however, that a two-field system was more suitable to some types of soil.

Economic Conditions
and the Life
of the Masses

balks at the head to allow for turning the plow. The manor court decided upon the crops to be grown and their rotation in the fields. A limited amount of meadowland, enclosed for the hay harvest and divided between the cultivators by lot, rotation, or other custom, provided winter feed for animals. The untilled area, rough grazing and woodland, provided permanent pasture onto which the villagers turned their cattle, sheep, and swine to graze.

Arable land was divided into two parts: the demesne or share of the manorial overlord, sometimes separate, sometimes scattered through open fields; and the villeinage, the small holdings of the peasantry. The word "villein" originally meant merely the inhabitant of a vill, that is, a hamlet, village, or even a small town. In time it came to mean an unfree or servile tenant who owed the lord works or services, who was legally bound to the soil and unable to leave either the manor or its lord.

The greater part of the land in villeinage was held in whole or half virgates. A "virgate," or a quarter of a hide[2] of arable land, made up, in theory, a farm sufficient to support a peasant family. They held it in the

---

[2] An area of land of about 100 acres, or as much as could be tilled with one plow. Its extent varied somewhat in different parts of the country.

form of strips scattered in the open fields. It was a unit of value rather than of pure areal measurement and could, therefore, vary in different districts according to the fertility of the soil. Roughly speaking, however, it can be equated with about thirty acres of arable and meadowland together with grazing rights over the manorial communal waste.

The holders of full virgates (some, of course, held more) were freemen and villeins and, whether free or servile, were, from the economic point of view, the socially superior peasant class. Below them were the bordars and the cottars, some of whom held as little as five acres or even less. Apart from slaves in some areas and a few craftsmen, these classes performed the agricultural work of the manor. Besides cultivating their own lands, they cultivated the lord's by a system of labor services: for a full virgate, they contributed two or three days' labor each week on the demesne and boon works—additional labor for a few days at the crises of the agrarian year, the spring and autumn plowings and the hay and grain harvests. Besides these services, they made small quarterly payments in money and, at various seasons, a large number of dues in kind—hens, eggs, bushels of oats or barley. Bordars and cottars occupying less land owed proportionately less in services and probably provided a pool of wage labor.

Manorial Organization and the Villages

It is not easy to picture either the natural state of England during the earlier Middle Ages or the various stages of development which slowly and gradually led to the classical form of the manor. As noted earlier,[3] most English villages came into existence between the fifth century and the compilation of Domesday Book in 1087. However, there is little archaeological evidence to tell us what they were like, compared with findings of Romano-British settlements. Abandoned Roman sites have been a gift to the archaeologists. Most Anglo-Saxon villages, having been continuously occupied to the present day, are closed to their pick and spade. A few which have been excavated show settlements of a very rough and primitive type indeed. Nor can archaeology tell us very much about Anglo-Saxon farming methods: only one plow and one plowshare have so far been recovered from the soil. All we can say is that groups of people, with no real scientific understanding of agriculture and with only the most basic and primitive of implements, faced the formidable task of clearing vast areas of forest. The Roman occupation of northwestern Europe had been thin. Consequently, these provinces still formed a forest culture of unreclaimed woodland, scrub, and marsh. The forest of Andredsweald, covering parts of Kent and Sussex, is said to have been 120 miles long and 30 miles wide. In the

[3] See p. 28.

pre-Viking period it swarmed with bears, wolves, wild boar, wild cattle, horses, beaver, and deer. The centuries from A.D. 600 to 1250 were the great age of deforestation, the gradual, heroically arduous, but in the end, inexorable encroachment of the arable on the wilderness.

Historians once claimed that Anglo-Saxon communities of men roughly free and equal worked the first herculean miracles of colonization and settlement, that social inequalities developed between the period of the sixth-century invasion and the Norman Conquest of 1066, that the manor in its fully fledged form was a comparatively late result of this social transformation. Such theories are only partially acceptable. Differences there must have been from the very earliest times. Although the invading Anglo-Saxon war bands spoke a more or less similar language— some variant of a Teutonic dialect—it is far more doubtful whether they came to England with similar economic experiences. A few had been in fairly close contact with the northern provinces of the Roman empire; others knew no more of its culture than the loot from sporadic piratical raids. The settlers were motley and diversified groups; from the very beginning, they lived in graded and unequal communities. They chose their kings and leaders from men of noble blood, who in turn had their followings of "ceorls," or common freemen. Captives brought in their train or native Roman-Britains they degraded into slavery. About 10 percent of the population remained slaves at the time of Domesday Book. We know something of these inequalities as early as the Laws of King Ine of Wessex in A.D. 688. One law states that if a lord demands labor services as well as rent he must provide his tenant with a house. Unfortunately, the law specifies neither the rent nor the work involved, but it certainly shows that even this early the law had sanctified some form of servile relationships. It seems clear, therefore, that many of the Anglo-Saxon village settlements must have supported their lords and aristocrats; it was hardly the free democratic society of the nineteenth-century Germanic imagination.

For many centuries, lordship and subordination formed the basic ties of discipline and social order in the English community. Even as early as Ine's time, there seems to be no doubt that the average man was under a lord and that economic, as distinct from social and legal, dependence upon lords steadily increased. This drift of the peasantry to diminished freedom had two main causes: first, the hazards of a society where standards of public order were always low drove the little man to seek the protection of the great man—a tendency reinforced by grants of royal jurisdiction to great estate owners; second, the effects of warfare on an agrarian economy always, through its low standard of productivity, near the margin of subsistence.

In a community where violence was normal and the formal organs of justice primitive, the patronage of a man of reputation and power in the neighborhood was always a powerful sanction against the aggressions of

unscrupulous neighbors. The earlier wars between the various small kingdoms and later the horrible devastations inflicted by the Scandinavian invasions have already been described. During these weary years of continued
devastation, burning, and looting, the small farmer, his crops destroyed,
harassed by debt and clemmed by famine, would commend himself to a
great man who could give him food, security, and protection. A Durham
document of the late tenth century even refers to free peasants who sold
themselves into slavery to obtain food. Lastly, the Danegeld, the famous tax
first levied to bribe off the invaders, became a crushing burden. According
to the Anglo-Saxon *Chronicle*, the sums taken varied from £10,000 in 991
to £82,000 in 1018. Still imposed after the Norman Conquest, in 1084 it
amounted to six shillings on every hide, about a third of the value of the
land, or to adopt another comparison, the price of three oxen. The tax was
heavy enough to destroy the independence of whole sections of society.
Peasants unable to raise their contribution to the geld appealed to richer
men for assistance. In return, they were obliged to commend themselves,
surrender their land, and accept some degree of servitude. It seems that a
society of this kind, whose margin of prosperity is small and which is
severely threatened by external dangers, becomes less and less free as time
goes on. By the time of the Norman Conquest, lordship and dependent
tenure prevailed over most of England. Feudalism in the economic sense—
that is, "the cultivation of land by the exercise of rights over persons"—was
already there and it continued to develop for another two and a half
centuries.

In this sphere, perhaps, the Norman Conquest was not such a dividing
line as it was in other ways: at most, the pace of certain tendencies may
have been somewhat accelerated. A few areas suffered badly. William's line
of march from Hastings to Dover and thence to London was badly devastated, but apart from this southeastern England suffered hardly at all. The
king again deliberately harried parts of Devon, Staffordshire, Cheshire,
Derbyshire, and Yorkshire after revolts in these areas in 1069–70. The effects of the devastation of Yorkshire were particularly acute. A comparison
of values for 1066 and 1086 in Domesday Book gives the West Riding in
1086 as worth just half its value of twenty years earlier, the North
Riding between a quarter and a fifth, and the East Riding as slightly more
than a quarter of its former value. Nor do these figures record the full extent
of the devastation for there had been a good deal of resettlement, for both
economic and strategic reasons, since the original harryings. Elsewhere, the
Norman aristocracy was too interested in exploiting its new estates to
slaughter the population out of sheer military intoxication and blood lust.
The peasantry, after all, suffered considerably less than the expropriated
Anglo-Saxon aristocracy. Their new owners may well have exploited some
estates more harshly, and some depression there certainly was. In 1066
there had been 900 "sokemen"[4] in Cambridgeshire. By 1086 their numbers

---

[4] Men commended to a lord and subject to his court but otherwise free.

had fallen to only 213. On the other hand, the large slave population (it was particularly prominent in the southwest) tended to disappear and, within a century of the Conquest, had vanished completely. Serfs, supporting themselves on their own bits of land, were probably easier to deal with.

The status of the rest of the population—the villani, the bordars, and the cottars—was complicated by the difference, and probably growing confusion, between legal and economic criteria. By this time differences of status among the village populations had become extremely complicated, a matter of great concern for the growing race of lawyers who were often bewildered by these varieties in peasant conditions. An obsessive passion for definition consumed the new common lawyers of the twelfth and thirteenth centuries. While they developed new modes of protection for the rights (particularly the property rights) of free men, they more and more denied access to the nascent royal courts to peasants bearing any taint of servile dependence, thus, in the course of time classifying all men not wholly free as villeins and profoundly changing the meaning of the word. At the same time, they tended to extend some of the more extreme disabilities of the former slaves to other "villeins" descended from original freemen, thus totally confusing the two to the disadvantage of the villein tenant who had been burdened originally only with lighter services.[5]

Convenient as it is to speak of the manor as the typical agrarian form, a kind of economic model, to do so gives an impression of undue simplicity. The natural division of the country into the highland and lowland zones still produced distinctions as it had earlier produced them in Roman times. The manor was a reality in the lowland zones of central and southern England, the area of champaign country; that is, open fertile plains suitable for grain growing. Even here, however, Domesday Book reveals that manors and villages did not usually coincide. In the eastern part of this area large villages with a single manor and a single lord were rare. Some villages had two or more, even as many as five, lords. Croyland Abbey, a rich monastic house of the second rank, possessed approximately fifty estates in east central England. Apart from Croyland itself, the manor included the whole village in only two cases. Elsewhere, Croyland shared the village territory with other lords and held one manor contiguous with those of other lords. On the other hand, there are examples of manors, like the Bishop of Winchester's estate at Taunton, where the manor covered several villages and hamlets.

Even within this champaign area there could be wide variations from the type. Owing to differences in soil, villages only a few miles apart could differ markedly in both their agricultural practices and their social structure. The southern half of Warwickshire, south of the River Avon, known to

---

[5] In some estate descriptions, the difference may be preserved in the terms "nativi" and "villani" and in later legal theories distinguishing between "villeins in gross" and "villeins regardant." Confusion was also confounded by the fact that villein tenements could be held by men who were not villeins by birth.

contemporaries as the Felden, was manorial, with a preponderance of grain crops; in the northern part, the Wealden, a far greater proportion of the land was devoted to grazing, and, therefore, labor services were lighter. Moreover, over wide areas geographical factors produced an entirely different economy For example, in Sherwood Forest—an "island" within the manorialized lowlands—open fields hardly existed. (Sherwood Forest was in the middle of Nottinghamshire, typical champaign country, where Laxton, one of the few open-field villages that still remain, is carefully preserved as a museum piece.) Each village possessed a little enclosed land, either arable or pasture, but over the greater part of the area sheep and cattle grazed, together with the royal deer. From time to time the villagers enclosed different pieces of land called "brecks," or "breaks," which they cultivated for a few years and then returned to pasture. The major labors of Sherwood were typical of a forest area: the specialized occupations of charcoal burning and pig breeding.

In other parts of the country, over much wider areas, differences were even more fundamental. The East Anglian Fens were waterlogged marshes scattered, here and there, with islands of very fertile soil. On some of the islands like Ely, the site of the great monastery and the Norman cathedral, a complete field system flourished. On the marshes surrounding these islands, fish and fowl—the products of the waters—and cattle dominated the Fenland economy and the lives of its people. Some villages netted as many as 20,000 eel in a year, and Ely Abbey accepted them in astronomical numbers for rent. Many a monk must have grown acutely bored at the constant reappearance of this rather oily fish on the refectory table. Although too wet for sheep, the Fens were a great pasture area for cattle, so well organized that villages had worked out complex arrangements for sharing grazing land when it had sufficiently dried out from the winter floods. Here the dangers of the waters, not the grain crops of the open fields, dominated peasant lives. The lands of the Fen had to be kept dry and free from flooding; the maintenance of the dykes and the drainage system compelled eternal labor if the whole system were not to be endangered. Moreover, drainage work was often beyond the means of any one individual manor or village, so that villages had to combine their efforts to control the water. In some areas as many as twenty-two or twenty-three large villages combined to cope with the water problem. Obligations to the land itself and the safety of the whole community, therefore, took precedence over any obligations and services to particular lords. Faced by relentless natural forces, lords had to yield claims which they would have enforced upon tenants in more favorable circumstances.

The narrow valleys in the hills and mountains of the West and the uplands of a great deal of the North left no room for large open fields. Their peoples practiced a pastoral economy or cultivated small individual farms. Sheep breeding called for less labor than grain production, and during the thirteenth century and after pastoral farmers and their families took to domestic industry, particularly spinning and weaving. Again, villages on the seacoast rarely conformed to the classical manorial type. Many tenants of Battle Abbey cultivated no more than an acre or two of land and paid their dues to the monks in fish.

Racial origins may have been responsible for differences in other areas. Although the soil and configuration of the landscape were suitable for the development of the classical field system, the agrarian organization of Kent differed greatly from that of the midland plains. It never became highly manorialized. Although Kentish organization was in law manorial, this legal framework did not affect agricultural practice as much as it did elsewhere. Such few labor services that existed were mainly of a nonservile character. The tenants were very nearly free. Some historians have tried to explain the origins of this surprisingly free society of Kent by geographical factors. They argue that, as Kent lay across the main trade route from London to the Continent and also supplied the London market with food, developing trade early stimulated the growth of a more intensive money economy which acted to dissolve the manor earlier than in other regions. As we shall see later, however, the growth of personal freedom did not always coincide with the growth of trade: sometimes the reverse applied. If these arguments are valid for Kent, a similar development should have occurred in other counties, notably Essex and Hampshire, which were also on trade routes to the Continent, yet very little freedom was to be found there. The explanation most probably lies in racial origins rather than in geography. Kent was originally settled by the Jutes, a distinct tribe, and Kentish freedom, and other peculiarities of Kentish tenure, may have resulted from the original differences of the conquerors developing in their own way.

Differences of ownership as well as variations in terrain and racial origins also caused distinct variations in methods of exploiting estates, even in the highly manorialized parts of England. A large monastery, for example, required a good deal of food for its numerous inmates. Many monastic manors, therefore, grew food for immediate consumption. This, to some extent, isolated many of them from the effects of growing markets. The uniformity of old ideas about the manor was due largely to the fact that the pioneer economic historians worked almost exclusively with a limited number of records from great Benedictine monasteries. However, individuals, not communities, owned the episcopal and great lay estates: individuals who, although they maintained enormous households, wanted money and luxury goods which the sale of farm products could buy. Such estates, if favorably situated, were very much open to the effects of growing markets in the towns. And some of these estates were great indeed: the earldom, later the duchy, of Lancaster contained over 500 manors, scattered all over the country; the duchy of York in the fifteenth century, well over 400. Even when trade and exchange were at their lowest, it was obviously impossible to run such a complex of estates for domestic consumption. They were always run for money, and, with cash revenues much in mind their successive owners changed their organization to meet changing economic circumstances, switching from leasing to tenants to a combination of leasing and direct exploitation in the late twelfth and thirteenth centuries and back again to a leasehold system after about 1340.

Finally, there were the estates of the smaller laymen, the men between the rank of peasant and rich lords. These were knights and esquires, some with as little as 160 acres, not much more prosperous than the most substantial of the peasants. The Russian historian Kosminsky, who carried out an investigation of midland England from the Hundred Rolls of 1274,[6] found in this largely manorialized area great differences of exploitation on different types of estates. At this particular time, on some large estates, direct farming—to a great extent based on villein labor—played an important and leases only a secondary role. On the other hand, on the small and medium-size estates, money rents rather than labor services decidedly predominated in the obligations of the villeins, and the lords cultivated their demesnes much more with wage labor.

We have already traced the process through which a great part of the peasantry lost its freedom in Anglo-Saxon times and later. But time never stood still in agrarian organization. Though still developing in its legal aspects, economically the manor began to dissolve almost as soon as it was formed. In many areas for a century after 1066 a steady process of dissolution went on, and many labor services were commuted. With the low-level administrative techniques then available, it was difficult to manage large scattered estates, and the chronic violence of the Anglo-Norman period, followed by the disorders of Stephen's reign, made it even more difficult—though these problems were by no means peculiar to England. The process of leasing was well under way in France by the end of the twelfth century, in the Rhineland by the thirteenth.

In England, however, reaction was setting in during the second half of the twelfth century, a reaction which lay in two very much interconnected phenomena: the growth of a more intensive money economy and a vast growth in population. Expanding trade and commerce and growing population together brought about a greatly increased demand for agricultural products. Between 1087 and 1300 population increased from about 1.5 to about 3.7 million,[7] an increase so great that it began to press hard upon such food supplies as the acreage of land already under cultivation could produce, and a considerable expansion took place both in the arable land and in the number of centers for marketing its produce. During the thir-

---

[6] This covers Huntingdonshire and parts of Cambridgeshire, Bedfordshire, Buckinghamshire, Oxfordshire, and Warwickshire.
[7] Owing to inadequate data, all estimates of medieval population are hypothetical. This is one of the lowest estimates. The highest estimates claim an increase to over 6 million.

teenth century over 3,000 new charters were issued for local markets, and the king and other lords founded eighty-eight new towns. From most parts of England there is considerable evidence of "assarting," that is, internal colonization or the reclamation of hitherto uncultivated land for cropping. In the Norfolk Fenlands, in the "wapentake"[8] of Elloe, a land-hungry community reclaimed fifty square miles between 1170 and 1241, and the remaining parts of the dense forest of Arden were also being cleared at this time. Settlers moved back into the parts of Yorkshire which William the Conqueror had devastated, and in Devon, where at the time of Domesday Book cultivation had reached no higher than the 1,000-foot contour, for a short time in the thirteenth century it extended to land 1,300 feet above sea level. Men, after all, do not welcome a climb of several hundred feet to their work if more accessible sites are available.

Farm products commanded higher prices. The price of wheat more than trebled between 1160 and 1300. The prices of nonfoodstuffs rose less steeply—a more or less sure indication of population pressure. Estates with convenient access to urban markets grew strikingly in value. Between 1087 and 1220 the revenues in 272 baronial estates had increased by 60 percent. An approximately equal increase occurred during the next thirty years, and even then revenues continued rising, though more slowly. In 1066 the Bishop of Ely drew a net income of £484 a year from his estates. By 1171–72 the income had increased to £920 and by 1298–99 to £2,250, a fivefold increase in income as against a threefold increase in wheat prices. The successive bishops of Ely were obviously growing steadily richer. An unknown proportion of this increase came from assarting, but much certainly from a combination of enhanced rents and the direct exploitation of the episcopal demesnes.

So a slow, but cumulative, rise in population accompanied by a steady rise in prices over a long period made it safe for landlords to invest in their estates and work their demesnes themselves. A considerable labor supply was needed for the direct exploitation of large estates. Farm labor for grain crops is a highly seasonal affair, with much of the year's work concentrated in a few weeks.[9] Despite the rise in population, in some areas in the late eleventh and early twelfth centuries there may not have been sufficient wage labor available at an economic price to meet the rising demand. Whether moved by such considerations or merely by highly conservative instincts, some landlords reimposed labor services which they had earlier allowed their villeins to commute. On the Ely estates, the demesnes expanded rapidly from the latter part of the twelfth century to at least the end of the third quarter of the thirteenth, and the bishops exacted a 10 percent increase in the work demanded from their villeins. Again, on three

---

[8] This term was used in areas of Scandinavian settlement and is roughly the same area known in other parts of the country as the hundred.
[9] See p. 4.

manors, Bromley, Stretton, and Burton in Staffordshire and Derbyshire belonging to Burton Priory, an early twelfth-century survey describes the tenants as villeins subject to full labor dues. A generation later, the Priory had leased most of its demesnes to former villeins who had now become *censuarii*, or rent-paying tenants, but by the thirteenth century the tenants were bitterly complaining in the royal courts that their landlord was once again treating them as villeins and demanding labor services. On other estates where there may have been a better supply of labor commutation went on unchecked. The county of Suffolk saw both processes at work: Suffolk was near London; through the ports of Harwich and Ipswich it had connections with the prosperous Flanders trade. On some estates there was a reaction to manorialism; on others commutation continued. In this way, Suffolk was a microcosm of the rest of England. The growth of trade and commerce did not automatically lead to greater freedom. The development of freedom was much more dependent upon the state of the local labor supply and the power of the landlord.

So, in the later twelfth and thirteenth centuries great landlords found conditions suitable and profitable for exploiting more of their estates directly. Such conditions, however, proved to be ephemeral. From the second quarter of the fourteenth century, earlier in some places, the dissolution of the demesne economy and its labor services began again until, by the 1390s, most great landlords drew the bulk of their income from rents. This time the change was permanent, despite the attempts of some landlords to reverse the process again in a period of acute labor shortage after the Black Death (1349).

The Population Crisis and the Black Death

Before this came to pass, however, acute crisis had already stricken the country and its people, although, owing to conflicting and intractable data, historians are still furiously speculating over the details of the problem. The increase in population which had, for several generations, so augmented the wealth of the landlord class was, by the end of the thirteenth century, developing into a catastrophe of over-population, a Malthusian crisis. As the population was still so small compared with that of modern times, this contention may seem incredible at first. Different conditions, however, render it plausible enough. Some areas now fertile were then barren, others were wilderness. Southwestern Lancashire was mostly covered with spreading moss, and between 300,000 and 400,000 acres of the Fens, which, since they were drained in the seventeenth century, have provided some of England's most fertile arable land, were then the scene of the primitive fishing and fowling economy already described. Moreover, the productivity of even the best arable land was probably no more than about a ninth of what it is today. In addition, the land had to provide many commodities such as clothing, fuel, building materials, and the means of transport, which today are furnished by artificial fabrics and minerals.

In such preindustrial agrarian societies, there was always a crude ratio between the standard of living of the masses and the commodities which they could wring from the local soil. Once this ratio collapsed, disaster followed, for there were no means of supplying long-term shortages. Poor and expensive transport (the cost of grain doubled every hundred miles when transported by road) prohibited the long-distance movement of bulk supplies of food. In any case, even cheap transport would have made little difference, for industrial production was so low that such societies had nothing with which to pay for large supplies of imported food. By the early fourteenth century, famine conditions indicate that Malthusian crisis had become endemic over the whole of Europe. The frightful years from 1315 to 1317 produced an appalling death roll.[10] A generation later the Black Death of 1349 and the less mortal but still severe Grey Death of 1361 were so lethal probably because they struck a population whose resistance to epidemic disease had been seriously undermined by several decades of chronic malnutrition.

Yet in the end, the fearful mortality of the plague years—the population declined by about two-fifths between 1349 and the end of the century—was a blessing in disguise for the survivors: destroying the excess population, it restored a more favorable balance between food supplies and people. Much of the land brought under the plow at the height of the thirteenth-century boom had been marginal land, yielding very low returns for the labor put into it, and, after several years of cropping, its fertility rapidly declined. Although much of this land was now abandoned, its desertion did not, as some historians have too readily assumed, mean declining prosperity. As there were fewer to feed, such difficulty unprofitable territory was no longer needed. Although total agricultural output diminished to less in 1400 than it had been a century earlier, production per head of the population was certainly greater—this, more than total production, was the foundation of prosperity.

Remarkable changes followed the Black Death, changes which greatly improved the lot of the working population. Plague largely wiped out the pool of surplus labor on some estates, and the surviving villeins became more recalcitrant and much more successful in resisting the demands of their lords. Since the mid-thirteenth century there had been a number of violent, though scattered, peasant risings. This tradition of peasant resistance reached its violent climax in the famous revolt of 1381: resistance in the main to the efforts of the landowning classes to hold down wages (wage

[10] See p. 7.

labor had steadily been replacing services) though, in some areas, against labor services as well.

These new conditions resulted in a wider prosperity, but there is no conclusive evidence (as some writers have maintained) that the peasantry as a class waxed fat to the detriment of their landlords. Once again, there were wide local variations, and even variations between different manors on the same estate. Some estates, particularly in the Midlands, suffered a great decline in revenues, but others in more favorable areas maintained, and in some cases even increased, their profits. From this time on, techniques of estate management improved; in fact, some estates were considerably better managed than they had been in the earlier period of extensive leasing. Moreover, before the Black Death there had been a great excess of prospective tenants over the number of farms available. Such people were now ready and eager to take over vacant tenements, and the almost pathological desire of peasants to work their own land almost certainly helped to keep up the level of rents.

This new spate of leasing the great demesnes afforded greater opportunities to the smaller landowners, whether gentlemen of modest means or peasants who took up leases upon them—men whose more intimate knowledge of local markets and local conditions enabled them to exploit their opportunities more effectively than could absentee landlords. During the fifteenth century the lower ranks of English society were "in quiet and prosperous estate." The aristocratic French chronicler Jean Froissart, who spent a good deal of time at the English court, commented with sour distaste on the independence, not to say insolence, which this new prosperity induced. According to his interpretation of events, the peasants of 1381 revolted from all the confidence of prosperity, not from the miseries of poverty. Later, in a book written probably in exile in the late 1460s, Chief Justice Fortescue was at pains to contrast the liberal diet, good clothing, and generally comfortable lives of the English with the miseries of the French peasantry—and other evidence shows that he was not merely dreaming the nostalgic dreams of an emigré.[11] With the rapid commutation of labor services, villeinage ceased to be a significant economic force. The majority of villeins became copyholders; that is, for the most part they paid money rents for their tenements and acquired copies of the entries on the manorial court rolls where their obligations were set out.

At the same time, the new opportunities, as always, did not benefit all. Increasing flexibility led to greater differentiation among the peasantry itself. There had been an active peasant land market since at least as early as the thirteenth century, but stimulated by the changing conditions following upon the Black Death land sales and transfers brought about a far greater differentiation between the ranks of richer and poorer peasants.

---

[11] See pp. 126–27.

While the horrible misery of the late thirteenth century vanished, the more capable throve to the detriment of the less fortunate and the less efficient. Some men sold out to become landless laborers; others, leasing more and more land, became prosperous, substantial farmers, like Chaucer's Franklin, in whose house is "snowed of meat and drink." The manor of Apsley Guise shows the process at work remarkably well: in 1275 the tenants held more or less equal holdings of about fifteen acres each. By 1542 only three of these formerly standard tenements remained, while one prosperous farmer held sixty acres and three had accumulated as many as seventy-five.

Standard of Living of the Peasantry

One of the hardest things of all to reconstruct is the standard of living of these English peasants across the centuries. The first Anglo-Saxon settlements were very small, and the few that have been excavated reveal primitive huts of a very wretched type indeed. Some of the larger villages of the later Anglo-Saxon period certainly contained substantial timber buildings, but stone was rare except for churches, and even some of the cathedrals were built of wood. However, we know that as late as the eleventh century it was a large village which contained as many as thirty households, and even some with churches had as few as ten.

Their appearance is even more elusive. Very few of the homes of the people survive from the Middle Ages, owing to the "great rebuilding" of rural England between 1540 and 1640 when, with rising standards among the more prosperous farmers, most of the more durable medieval village houses were replaced, altered, or enlarged. Some of the very poorest people lived in round mud huts. None of these huts has survived, being too flimsy to last more than a few years. A more substantial and very common type was the "cruck" house, so called because its principal timbers curved from the ground to meet at the center and each pair was joined by a ridgepole which ran the whole length of the house, thus holding the crucks firmly together. This simple construction obviously severely limited internal headroom. Later, more prosperous people improved upon it by placing the crucks on vertical timbers, which formed corner and intermediate posts rising eight or ten feet from the foundations. Wattle and daub, cob (a mixture of clay and straw), or earth and mud filled the spaces. Wattle consisted of upright sticks with twigs woven in and out of them, upon which daub was then thrown until it was thick enough. Few peasant houses had more than two rooms: one for living, cooking, and eating, and one for sleeping. Glass windows were luxuries for the rich, and even they did not regard them as permanent fixtures: when families were not in residence, their windows were taken out and stored. A fire burned upon a hearth in the middle of the room, the smoke (or some of it) escaping through a louver in the roof.

Chaucer remarked of his poor widow's dwelling, "Full sooty was her hall and eek her bower." Furniture was rude and scanty—a chest, a table, and a few stools—and kitchen utensils were valuable enough to be mentioned in wills. Bags of straw or flock served for mattresses and logs of wood for pillows. Even in the late sixteenth century old-fashioned conservatives felt outraged when servants began to demand flock or feather pillows, and they thought the prevalence of chimneys unhealthy. Smoke, they claimed, was good for the lungs.

These huts—overcrowded, verminous, exiguously furnished, utterly comfortless—housed a peasant population excessively vulnerable to disease, browned and wrinkled by constant exposure to the sun and winds of the fields and the smoke-filled atmosphere of their squalid hovels. The contempt and scorn shown by aristocrat and burgher toward the peasantry were due in no small measure to the cruel distinction of their physical appearance. The emphasis in contemporary literature upon whiteness, paleness, and fairness as criteria of physical beauty is an index of how difficult these were to retain beyond the years of early youth.

Evidence from the manor of Farnham about the end of the thirteenth century gives some idea of the diet of the middling (by no means the poorest) members of the community. Farnham belonged to the Bishop of Winchester, one of the richest prelates in Europe. Its standard of productivity was perhaps rather lower than that of some other villages, but otherwise it was in no way unusual. Many of its villeins had commuted their services for money payments in 1258, but the bishop still demanded services from others. The standard villein tenement consisted of about thirty-two acres: small enough for the villein family to work without hired help. Roughly speaking, this area would have produced sufficient grain to provide a family of five with about eighteen or nineteen two-pound loaves a week (more than half of them made of barley) and about eighteen gallons of very weak ale. About a third of a peasant's grain crop went to the making of ale, and even as late as the seventeenth century a seventh of the total national income was spent upon it. Oats provided pottage and oat cakes, and rations for probably three beasts. As to meat and animal products, such a family might eat an ox if one died from natural causes during the year (oxen were generally far too valuable to slaughter for food), perhaps thirty pounds of mutton a year, four or five pigs, a little cheese and butter, a few chickens and eggs, peas, beans and onions, but few other vegetables, and such fruit as their orchards and the hedgerows yielded.

At best, it was a monotonous and deficient diet. Today, social workers would consider it vile by the standards of even meager welfare programs—and this was the standard of living of one of the more prosperous peasant families, the tenants of about thirty-two acres, or a full virgate. One result of the growing population, however, had been, by the end of the thirteenth century, the subdivision of such holdings. On 104 manors scattered over eight estates in different parts of the county, tenants with only a quarter virgate or less formed at least 45 percent of the total population. Economic historians argue vigorously about the amount of land necessary to keep a family above the subsistence level at that time: their estimates vary from about eight to sixteen acres. How such people lived baffles the imagination. Such meager holdings could hardly support them, unless they hired themselves out for wages for part of the time, but in the later thirteenth century, the demand for labor seems to have been too small to absorb more than a minority of this increasing group of the deprived. At Waltham, in the mid-thirteenth century, at least 16 percent of the tenants could be called paupers, their holdings were so small. On another of the Bishop of Winchester's manors, Witney in Oxfordshire, many people were exempted from tiny contributions to papal taxation on account of their poverty: they were so poor that they did not even possess a beast worth thirty pence. Such conditions have led a recent author to write of "the thirteenth-century English peasantry as consisting largely of smallholders leading a wretched existence on an inadequate number of acres."[12]

One of the most moving passages in fourteenth-century literature is the description of a plowman's family in the poem *Pierce the Plowman's Crede:*

> As I went by the way, weeping for sorrow, I saw a poor man hanging on to the plough. His coat was of a coarse stuff which was called cary; his hood was full of holes and his hair stuck out of it. As he trod the soil his toes stuck out of his worn shoes with their thick soles; his hose hung about his hocks on all sides and he was all bedaubed with mud as he followed the plough. He had two mittens, scantily made of rough stuff, with worn-out fingers and thick with muck. This man bemired himself in mud almost to the ankle, and drove four heifers before him that had become feeble, so that men might count their every rib as sorry-looking they were.
>
> His wife walked beside him with a long goad in a shortened cote-hardy looped up full high and wrapped in a winnowing-sheet to protect her from the weather. She went barefoot on the ice so that the blood flowed. And at the end of the row there lay a little crumb-bowl, and therein a little child covered with rags, and two two-year-olds were on the other side, and they all sang one song that was pitiful to hear: they all cried the same cry—a miserable note. The poor man sighed sorely and said, "Children be still!"

This poem was written (*c*. 1394) after the Black Death, when more land was available, the worse miseries were past, and rural conditions had notably improved. Yet in spite of the strictures of Jean Froissart and the later eulogies of Sir John Fortescue, the lives of many of the poorer country folk remained anything but comfortable: by any standards, their lives were grim, austere, and deprived.

[12] J. Z. Titow, *English Rural Society, 1200–1350* (London and New York, 1969), p. 93.

Life in the Towns

So far we have said nothing of the towns—deliberately, for no more than a tenth of the population lived in towns, and in this period, the proportion grew no larger. With the exception of London, and possibly one or two other places, the town populations fluctuated roughly as the population of the country increased or declined. London apart, the towns always retained, in spite of their walls, a distinctly rural atmosphere. As late as the sixteenth century the weavers of Norwich (by then the second largest city in the kingdom) were still forbidden to work at their craft during the harvest: the needs of the fields took precedence over industry.

The origin of towns—or boroughs, as they were technically called—is obscure and controversial. Some certainly began as administrative centers of the countryside before the development of the shire and the hundred. Many grew up as part of the defensive system constructed against the Danes in the ninth century, but, not all of these, by any means, developed into prosperous towns. A site chosen solely for strategic reasons was not *ipso facto* suitable for the development of trade. Partly in an attempt to limit theft in a disorderly society, partly to make certain of royal revenues from tolls, shortly after A.D. 900 Edward the Elder issued a law prohibiting buying and selling outside boroughs. Had this law been successfully enforced (which it apparently was not), it would have greatly stimulated the growth of the boroughs.

After the Norman Conquest there was a great expansion of commerce, and the twelfth century, an age conspicuous for the growth of towns all over Europe, saw a whole crop of royal (and some seigneurial) charters granted to English towns. Henry I granted 17; Henry II, 75; and Richard I and John, 250 between them. Towns and their inhabitants had very different needs from those of the countryside and the feudal classes, and charters meant privileges, exemptions from normal practice, which allowed them to develop in their own way. Though details, of course, varied from town to town, these franchises everywhere followed a similar pattern.

A privilege ardently sought after was "burgage tenure," the power freely to alienate land. With this concession won, burgesses were freer than either knights or villeins. Feudal tenants and villeins could alienate their lands only within the most restrictive conditions; townsmen could now buy and sell urban land so freely that they could use it as security for credit in commercial transactions. Next came the greatly desired concession (often bought for a heavy price in cash) of the *firma burgi*, the right of the town to *farm* for a fixed annual sum the dues and tolls due to the king or some other lord, a concession much valued as a protection against unexpected exactions and freedom from constant, exasperating intervention by royal or seigneurial officials. The grant of the *firma burgi* stimulated, if it did not originate, municipal self-government, for it meant that in order to collect and pay over such dues the town must develop its own internal organization. Lastly, towns gained valuable jurisdictional privileges and the right to hold their own courts, over which elected officials presided and in which they applied the *law merchant*, an international, if at first somewhat vague, corpus of law developing to deal with commercial transactions: more quickly and much more flexibly, and using methods of procedure and proof by witnesses more rational and modern than those of the common law of the land. Chartered towns developed such distinctive characteristics of their own, characteristics so alien to the tone of the rural, knightly society about them that they have been called "oases of freedom in a desert of feudalism."

Their commercial privileges in particular came to be generally expressed in the form of the "Gild Merchant." By the middle of the twelfth century, many town charters included this particular institution, the earliest known grant being in a charter to the little Cotswold town of Burford (*c.* 1070–1107). About half of the known chartered towns possessed it, although it was not essential to development and even major cities like London and Norwich got on very well without it.

The Gild Merchant meant, in effect, that its members, always the major inhabitants of the borough, enjoyed a monopoly, free from tolls, of all commercial transactions within it. Nongildsmen could buy and sell wholesale to gildsmen only, and that again only upon the payment of fairly heavy dues. Retail trade they could not undertake within the town at all. In theory, such privileges were supposed to work for the good of all, ensuring an adequate supply of food and other goods for the townsfolk. Fear of dearth was a constant urban nightmare, dominating most municipal legislation. Gildsmen, therefore, paid for their highly lucrative privileges with certain severe restrictions on their own freedom of action. Officials of the gild examined all goods offered for sale to enforce minimum standards of quality. Offenders against such standards might be expelled from the gild either temporarily or permanently. The members had to bear their share of the common financial burdens of the community, or, as the phrase went, "to be at scot and lot." Such financial burdens could at times be very heavy: a sudden call for funds to repair or extend the town walls, for example, must have strained the purse of many a gildsman, even to the dislocation of some of his planned commercial ventures.

The first craft gilds appeared almost simultaneously with the Gild Merchant. Henry I (1100–35) granted their first charter to the London weavers. Generally speaking, however, the craft gilds, associations of specialized artisans, represented a somewhat later stage of development. They came into being when demand for a particular article in the town and its surrounding district rose to a level high enough to support a group of men engaged in its production. With a level of production, still minute by modern standards, but expanding, the craft gilds marked the first stage in industrial organization and specialization, of greater efficiency through the division of labor: first, a small commercial class expressing itself through the Gild Merchant, now a small industrial class expressing itself in the craft gilds.

As usual, new specialized developments did not occur without opposition from vested interests. The Gild Merchant represented the commercial oligarchy of the whole town, the craft gilds particular interests within the town. When these narrow sectional interests tried to enforce their own complete control over their crafts, they often made rules conflicting with the interests of both the established commercial oligarchy and the well-being of the wider community. Bitter disputes then inevitably occurred. Depending upon local circumstances, such disputes might, or might not, be an expression of class conflict. In early twelfth-century London, the weavers paid the royal Exchequer the enormous sum of £12 a year for freedom from tolls. They lived in their own quarter which the city officers were forbidden to enter and raised their taxes through their own officers. In a very medieval way, they were trying to establish a second privileged community within a privileged community, a franchise within a franchise: the action of a wealthy sectional group trying to escape the common rules and obligations in their own interests. On this occasion the conflict was constitutional rather than economic. In many smaller communities, however, the craft gilds did represent artisans opposed to an oligarchy which tried to keep them under control, whether in the name of the general good or, less creditably, in the interests of the more prosperous. In the end the struggle resulted in the triumph of the town authorities. In Norwich, for example, in 1286, the municipal authorities chose two members every year from each gild to search four times a year for defective wares and present them to the city bailiffs for condemnation. Any ordinance which the gilds made had to be approved by the city authorities, who, at various times, fined the Cobblers, the Saddlers, and the Fullers for establishing gilds without permission.

Romantic historians very much idealized the craft gilds as seats of a primitive, harmonious social democracy, seeing in them not later ideas of unrestricted gain but an ideal life of subsistence according to a man's social status. A man's profits should be limited by his needs. His needs were roughly defined by his position in society. Society consisted of a number of groups, each with its own appropriate standard of living recognized by long-established conventions. The trading groups themselves were thus supposed to have worked for equality within their own conventional standard.

The craft gilds were democratic in that they were composed of equal, independent artisans. A boy entered his future trade only by serving an apprenticeship to a master; once out of his apprenticeship, he became a journeyman and, ultimately, a master craftsman himself. Class distinction within the group was utterly unknown. Apprentices and journeymen lived in their master's house, forming part of his family circle. This extended family lived and worked in a single, highly intimate, domestic unit, the modern separation between the family and its place of work being utterly unknown. Strict adherence to these ideals prevented wide differences in prosperity and the growth of capitalism, for gild regulations forbade masters to increase their output by taking an undue number of apprentices and journeymen. The Shearmen of London and the Worsted Weavers of Norwich allowed no more than four apprentices to each master.

Limited economic circumstances, however, rather than adherence to any consciously high-minded ideals, produced this supposedly altruistic atmosphere. The market conditions of a multitude of small towns, towns with a population of a few hundred people and a rural market limited by a radius of a few miles, forced such regulation upon the craft members: markets in which craftsmen could work only for customers they personally knew, where consumption was limited and more or less roughly known. Under such conditions the gild system was not only feasible, it was essential. Because the demand was so limited, only a given number of people could be allowed to trade, and apprenticeship had to be restricted because there was little or no scope for the expansion of individual businesses. Restricted conditions, not opportunity, produced a rough equality within privileged groups.

Such conditions obviously did not apply everywhere, or to all trades. Some towns never grew large enough to progress to even this modest degree of specialization and organization. The trades of Liverpool as late as 1378, for example, show only five fishermen, four drapers, four bootmakers, two tailors, and a tanner: two tailors could hardly form a gild. Shipbuilding and iron smelting took place outside the towns; neither of these trades seems to have been organized in gilds. The highly skilled craft of the stonemasons had its own peculiar organization in lodges as the masons moved across the countryside from castle to cathedral, from cathedral to abbey, wherever the erection of a great building happened to provide them with work.

Again, the classical organization of the gild vanished as soon as a town developed more than the restricted, familiar, local market. Gilds of London and the large seaports which bore the familiar craft names developed from groups of artisans into companies of speculating merchants with wide international connections. By the late thirteenth century the gilds of London —which later became the twelve great livery companies, under the names Mercers, Grocers, Drapers, Tailors, and so on—had become groups of men who traded in any commodity on which they could make a profit. Wherever towns produced goods, particularly cloth, for which there was an international demand, there developed a *grande industrie* totally alien in spirit and organization from the petty craft production of a local market town.

The small craftsman was obviously incapable of selling his goods directly to foreign customers hundreds of miles away. In these circumstances either general merchants or those engaged in the finishing trades, rather than in basic production, gained control of markets, or a minority of the richer gildmasters threw out the tools of their trade and turned merchant to specialize in marketing the goods of other craftsmen. Here a notable cleavage split the merchants from the lesser members of the gilds. The richer members became large-scale employers of labor and many journeymen could no longer aspire to become masters but remained forever dependent upon others. By the mid-thirteenth century, and probably earlier, merchants and the richer gild members monopolized this middleman role between producer and consumer; the producer, the master craftsman, in varying degrees lost his independence, becoming no more than a wage earner paid on piece-rates, although still working in his own home and, if a weaver, on his own loom.

Craft Gilds and the Cloth Industry

This more advanced type of organization became most prominent in cloth production. Woolen cloth was England's only major export. From the end of the fourteenth to the mid-seventeenth century, it made up at least 90 percent of the country's total exports. Although the production of cloth figures prominently in most books, its importance should not be exaggerated. About 1400 cloth production for export employed no more than about 17,000 to 20,000 people, calculated on a full-time basis, or less than 1 percent of the total population. England was still an overwhelmingly agrarian economy. The trade's significance lies mainly in its new organization and its effect upon the lives of a minority.

In the Middle Ages weavers everywhere produced coarse cloth for local consumption, but from the eleventh century onwards the production of fine luxury cloths for export rapidly advanced in two major centers, Flanders and Florence. These luxury industries required wool of exceptionally fine quality, a quality available only from the sheep farmers of Burgundy, the Spanish peninsula, and England. Of these sources of supply, English wool was by far the most important.

Even in late Anglo-Saxon times the country's riches, so attractive to both the Danes and William the Conqueror, were probably derived in the main from its sheep flocks. It is hardly possible to exaggerate their significance. As Professor Eileen Power once expressed it, England's

> commerce and her politics alike were built upon wool. When her kings got themselves taken prisoner, like Richard I, the ransom was paid—with grumbling—out of wool. When they rushed into war with their neighbours, like

the three Edwards, the wars were financed and allies bought—with more grumbling—out of wool. . . . At home honest burgesses climbed upon wool into the ranks of the nobility, only outstripped in their progress there by the dishonest ones who arrived first. . . . The very Lord Chancellor plumped himself down on a wool sack, and the kingdom might have set on its great seal the motto which a wealthy wool merchant engraved on the windows of his new house.

> I praise God and ever shall
> It is the sheep hath paid for all.[13]

Everybody from serfs to great landowners kept sheep. In 1225 in the village of South Domerham 198 tenants owned 3,700 sheep between them. In 1259 the Bishop of Winchester had 29,000 in various flocks, and the new twelfth-century religious order, the Cistercians, introduced into England in 1128, founded its fortunes almost entirely upon sheep breeding. Toward the end of the thirteenth century there could have been as many as fifteen or eighteen million sheep in the country—four or five sheep for every human being.

With its wealth dependent upon the export of a primary raw material, England during the late thirteenth and early fourteenth centuries was almost an economic colony of the Netherlands and Italy, particularly Italy. Italian merchants advanced money on their crops to the great sheepowners, both lay and ecclesiastical. By Edward I's reign these Italian merchants commanded so much of the country's liquid wealth that they became the Crown's bankers and creditors. Loans to the Crown led to the grant of special privileges to Italians in the English customs system, and these, in turn, led to an increased Italian hold over English trade. Italian firms like the Riccardi of Lucca and the Frescobaldi, the Bardi, and the Peruzzi of Florence dominated the wool trade and the royal finances. When an over-extension of their business transactions in the 1330s brought the Bardi and the Peruzzi crashing to ruin, Edward III turned to groups of English merchants for loans, to form, after various experiments, the company of the Merchants of the Staple, which, in return for its financial services to the Crown, received a monopoly of the export of wool, with the exception of that carried to Italy; the Italian quasi-monopoly was being broken.

At least as early as Charlemagne's time, English cloth had been well-known in Europe. Information about it, however, is remarkably scanty. By the late twelfth and the early thirteenth century every town of any size had its weavers, and in some of the corporate towns their gilds were rich and powerful. Four towns in particular—Beverley, Lincoln, Stamford, and Northampton—produced fine quality cloths for export, and York, Louth, and Leicester, among others, slightly cheaper goods. By the middle of the thirteenth century Stamford cloth merchants had considerable dealings in

---

[13] E. Power, *The Wool Trade in English Medieval History* (Oxford, 1941), p. 17.

Italy, and Spanish merchants were dealing in cloth from most of the famous production centers. By this time, however, the Flemish industry was capturing the European markets for the finest types of cloth, and the English towns were finding it increasingly difficult to compete. The English industry, therefore, turned more and more to cheaper goods, produced in the countryside rather than in the older cloth towns.[14]

In the fourteenth century Flanders lost this predominance in the cloth trade, and England saw a great switch from the export of raw materials to the export of manufactured goods—from wool to cloth. Between 1353 and 1368 cloth exports grew at the amazing rate of 18 percent a year, and, after an intervening slack period, growth continued at 8 percent a year between 1380 and 1395. Between 1350 and 1400 exports grew fourfold. In spite of periodic slumps, they continued to grow during the fifteenth century. Before 1350 the highest export total for any one year was 10,325 cloths;[15] after 1383 no year fell below 20,000. By the 1470s exports totaled over 62,000, and the expansion continued steadily until the boom period of the mid-sixteenth century. Nor do these export figures tell the whole story. With growing prosperity at home after the Black Death, the peasantry could afford to spend a greater proportion of their incomes on goods other than food, particularly on textiles. A considerable, although unknown, expansion of the domestic market therefore accompanied this remarkable rise in exports.

Although helped by foreign circumstances—acute labor troubles in the Flemish cities and the growth of new markets, at first in Gascony and then, toward the end of the fourteenth century, in Toulouse, the Iberian peninsula, the Baltic region, and the Netherlands itself—much of this growth came from an almost accidental protection. Quite fortuitously royal policy profoundly changed English economic development through the stimulus of war taxation. The intermittent campaigns of the Hundred Years War, which began in 1337, were very expensive, and Edward III, among other methods, raised money by taxing very heavily his country's main export: raw wool. About half the proceeds of war taxation came from levies on wool, for a raw material vital to foreign industries was an ideal commodity on which to raise large sums of money. Such taxation angered exporters, and to a lesser extent wool growers, but they were, after all, a sectional interest. From Edward's point of view, it was less dangerous to annoy them than to provoke the wider resentment which taxation of the whole population would have brought upon the monarchy and its war policies. Although this may have depressed a little the prices paid to the wool growers, the Merchants of the Staple naturally passed on the tax as far as they could to their

---

[14] See pp. 123–24.
[15] The standard cloth measure for customs purposes was twenty-four yards long by one and a half to two yards wide.

foreign customers. As only wool which left the country bore the tax, the English weavers obtained their raw material free of this burden. The Flemish and Italian weavers, unable to turn to alternative supplies of comparable quality, had to pay the tax, plus the exporter's profit, plus the cost of transport abroad, so that, all told, they paid at least 33 percent more for their wool than Englishmen did. It is true that the government also taxed cloth, but the tax was derisory in comparison, only about 2 or 3 percent.

Three important results followed, or were at least connected with, this change. At this time the labor costs of manufactured goods made up at least half their value. The switch from the export of a raw material to the export of finished goods, therefore, meant a considerable increase in the value of English trade. Secondly, from the second quarter of the fifteenth century the demand for wool grew so great that estate owners, especially in the midland counties, enclosed arable land for sheep runs, depopulating whole villages in the process (between fifty and sixty villages and hamlets in Warwickshire alone had been depopulated by 1500), thus causing considerable social distress among the smaller peasantry. The process continued, though probably at a slower rate, in the early sixteenth century and profoundly disturbed Tudor governments and social thinkers. Lastly, cloth manufacture took on a new form of organization, which lasted until the introduction of the factory system during the Industrial Revolution.

By the mid-thirteenth century English high-grade cloth production could no longer meet Flemish competition. By the second half of the

Processes in the woolen cloth industry. *Left to right:* Weaving on a single loom (BM Egerton MS. 1894 f. 2); spinning with distaff, carding, and combing (BM Royal MS. 16GV f. 56); dyeing in the piece (BM Royal MS. 15EIII f. 269). (All courtesy of the British Museum.)

century merchants were looking to the products of the rural areas: cloths of somewhat lower quality and certainly cheaper in price owing to lower wages paid outside the towns, particularly in pastoral districts where the lighter demands of cattle raising left farming families free and eager to add to their incomes by part-time spinning and weaving. This slump in urban and the growth of rural production took place in most areas. The change was also stimulated, although at first probably only to a lesser extent, by a revolution in "fulling," one of the finishing processes in the manufacture of cloth, the process in which cloth was washed and cleaned. Originally, the cloth was put into enormous vats of water with fuller's earth, then bare-footed "walkers" trod it down until they had cleaned it of the filth and grease which it had acquired during the weaving process on the loom. Water power had been applied to corn milling for a long time, and now cloth became the first industry to harness the forces of nature. Fulling mills were set up in which heavy wooden hammers, driven by water power, replaced the walkers. Between 1185 and 1327 at least 130 to 150 fulling mills were built—and there must have been a great many more, as nearly all our knowledge of them comes from estates owned by the king and ecclesiastics.

To obtain their power, fulling mills could be established without difficulty only in districts of fast-flowing streams. The famous early centers like Beverley, Stamford, and Leicester were situated on the sluggish rivers of the broad eastern plains. Most of the new fulling mills were built in the West and the Northwest, though there were at least two in the London area. The mills probably became progressively more important in reducing costs in the period of higher wages after the Black Death. As Sir John Clapham pointed out, by the fifteenth century types of cloth that had become household words abroad no longer took their names from the old corporate towns, "but from newly risen towns or districts where the water flows strongly to the mills."[16] "Kendal Greens," "Cotswolds," "Stroudwaters" had ousted the earlier "Stamfords" and "Lincolns."

In many areas in the fourteenth century, particularly in the Southwest, Yorkshire, and East Anglia, there was something of a revival of the urban cloth industry from its former slump. About 1400, for example, Salisbury exported more cloth than the entire county of Wiltshire had exported in 1330. The more highly skilled and supervised industry of some of the towns may have concentrated upon the finer grades, while some of the rural areas produced only middle-grade and coarse varieties of cloth. Yet, urban or rural, the organization of the industry changed in roughly the same way: it became dominated by commercial entrepreneurs. In the greater towns the gilds split. The richer masters, who became known as the livery, and the journeymen, or pieceworkers, organized themselves in what came to be

---

[16] *A Concise Economic History of Britain* (Cambridge, Eng., 1957), p. 156.

known as yeomen gilds: gilds of workers to protect (rather inefficiently) the interests of those who could no longer become masters, who were destined to remain forever wage earners. Yeomen gilds were most prominent in London, but they existed in many other towns—Bristol, Coventry, York. They generally failed to maintain their independence, and if they were not suppressed they were generally absorbed into the gilds of merchants as subordinate bodies under the control of the employers. In the cloth trade (and in other trades in large towns), the growth of markets left the classical types of gilds outmoded as economic institutions—and the new rural industry grew up completely outside their regulations.

The great technical advance in fulling remained very much alone. No comparable advances took place in the two main processes of the industry, spinning and weaving. There, the enormous expansion in output was achieved by a simple multiplication of the traditional, unpowered units of production, the spinner with her distaff, and, from some time in the late twelfth century, her spinning-wheel, and the weaver with his loom. Workers until the days of the factory system continued to own these instruments, but in the later Middle Ages they lost their independence because they came to rely upon the merchant clothiers for their supplies of raw materials. In this intermediate stage of industrial organization, the worker, to use modern economic jargon, still owned the industry's fixed capital but lost control of its circulating capital. His loss of independence, however, was just as complete as if he had lost control of both. The capitalist merchant, the "clothier," as he came to be called, gave out wool to be spun into yarn, collected the yarn, and gave it out again to the weaver, thus by his command over the raw material dominating the industry and its small producers.

In the Yorkshire area, which mainly supplied the home market, the clothier was generally a master craftsman employing workmen in his own home, making four or five cloths, and then taking them for sale to local centers like Wakefield and Halifax, both rising to prosperity in the fourteenth and fifteenth centuries on the cloth trade. In the West Country and East Anglia, the great export areas, the clothier developed into an altogether different type: a rich capitalist organizing his raw materials, his out-workers, production and sales on a far larger scale. The Ulnagers' Accounts[17] for the 1390s show that in Coggeshall in Essex one man alone was responsible for 400 cloths and in the West at Barnstaple two clothiers paid on more than a thousand each and that nine others together accounted for another thousand. Such traders were obviously entrepreneurs organizing production for distant markets, not the old type of local master craftsmen. By 1515 the town (it was still legally a village) of Lavenham in Suffolk, with a thousand or so inhabitants, had so prospered upon its cloth industry that only twelve

---

[17] "Ulnage" was the tax on cloth.

communities in the whole country paid more in taxes. Its principal inhabitants were the Spring family, clothiers so rich that Thomas, who died in 1468, left 300 marks (£200) in his will for rebuilding Lavenham Church and tower—and this at a time when Sir John Fortescue remarked that £5 a year was a good cash income for a yeoman and many a country squire managed on less than £20 a year. Thomas's son, also Thomas, left another £300 for the tower and £200 for the repair of the roads around Lavenham, and his daughter married into the aristocracy (a sure sign of merchant wealth) to Aubrey de Vere, a son of the Earl of Oxford.

Summary

Roughly speaking, the Anglo-Saxon period was an age of pioneer toil in which settlers cleared the major forests and established the basic rural geography of England as it is today. It was also an age of intermittent violence and low-level production, which together gradually, but inexorably, depressed the peasantry toward varying degrees of servitude. The twelfth and thirteenth centuries, with their rapid growth of population and steeply rising prices, continued the now age-long pressure upon the forests and the wilderness. This world of enhanced prosperity for the landlord class and the more prosperous peasants ultimately ran into the ever-threatening peril of all preindustrial societies: a Malthusian crisis in which the growth of population outstripped the productive capacity of the arable land available.

Although it is hardly possible to magnify the immediate terrors and horrors of the Black Death, it brought renewed hope, providing more land and the possibility of higher standards of living for the survivors. Although total agricultural production declined, output per head of the population, the vital factor for prosperity among peasant and wage earner, increased. Moreover, a change in trade from the export of a basic raw material to the export of a manufactured product served, though, it is true, only marginally, to increase the country's wealth. Society had advanced a long way since men in the tenth century had sold themselves into slavery for food, and the wretched smallholders, so prominent in the late thirteenth century, were much reduced in number, many of their descendants having become modest copyholders.

Unfortunately, the new prosperity was, in origin, fortuitous. Based upon the irrational forces of nature rather than upon technological progress, it again began to decline as soon as those forces went into reverse with a new growth of population. Slowly under way by the 1430s, population began to grow rapidly from the 1460s. Significantly, the first proclamation against that Tudor horror, the sturdy beggar, dates from the 1470s. Demographers plausibly estimate that between the mid-fifteenth and the mid-seventeenth century population nearly doubled. So great an increase brought back in its inevitable train all the earlier problems, dislocations, and degradations. Landlords throve on rising rents, freeholders and the greater tenants on rising farm prices; smallholders and wage earners once more sank into abysmal poverty. By 1597, the year of Shakespeare's *Midsummer Night's Dream*, their standard of living had once again fallen to late thirteenth-century levels. Though Tudor England in the higher ranges of society supported an increasingly rich and varied culture, the more widely based prosperity of the later Middle Ages withered away—to revive permanently only in the nineteenth century upon the sounder basis of an industrial economy.

CHAPTER SEVEN

The growing prosperity of the upper ranks of the landowners and the merchants was but one aspect of the advances of the thirteenth century. Building upon the cruder structures of the twelfth century, the thirteenth was an age of remarkable, though, perhaps, in the final analysis somewhat frustrated, achievement. Old towns were growing; many new ones were deliberately founded. The gothic style which had begun to replace the romanesque in twelfth-century France now reached its most sophisticated, serene, and accomplished technical development in the building, during the first quarter of the century, of the great cathedrals of Rheims, Amiens, and Beauvais. St. Louis of France in three years (1245–48) erected the lantern-like Sainte-Chapelle in Paris to house his most precious relic—a fragment of the True Cross. The English adopted the new style a little later, with a tinge of provincial crudity compared with French perfection. The north-eastern parts of Salisbury Cathedral, the choir of Worcester, the nave of Lincoln, and the western end of Wells all rose from their foundations during the second quarter of the century. The abbey church of Westminster, the most glorious building of its day in England, was consecrated in 1269. Henry III, the "dilettante of genius" who commissioned and paid for it, was one of the greatest patrons of art ever to sit on the English throne—though, like his two most notorious successors in connoisseurship Richard II

The Thirteenth Century:
Baronial Revolt
and Royal Stalemate

and Charles I, he was a political failure. The combination of the aesthete and the statesman has rarely succeeded in English life.

The medieval church was now at the height of its prestige. In spite of the horrors of the Albigensian Crusade in southern France, Pope Innocent III (1198–1216) successfully began the repression of heresy as much by new pastoral efforts as by force. St. Thomas Aquinas, for the time at least, in his *Summa Theologica*, the great thirteenth-century synthesis of reason and faith, of Athens and Jerusalem, brilliantly countered the dangers with which the rediscovery of Aristotle's works threatened traditional orthodoxy. The ecclesiastical authorities welcomed and encouraged inspired and devoted pastoral workers in the vigorous new orders of the Mendicant Friars, the Franciscans, and the Dominicans. The Franciscans, especially, introduced a sweeter, gentler, more humane note into orthodox Christianity which strikingly contrasted with its somewhat grim, majestic, heroic atmosphere of earlier centuries, an appeal which they reinforced in a very practical way by evangelical work among the poorer sections of the population, particularly in the growing towns, which the predominantly aristocratic church of the twelfth century, to the danger of its own peace and security, had to a grave extent neglected.

At the same time, profounder studies of both Aristotle's political

Map of Medieval England.

works and of Roman law gave a new theoretical basis to political life and to ideas about the state, while monarchs in western Europe were also expanding their practical powers over their subjects' lives and resources. In the realms of law and government, the thirteenth century witnessed a progress from vagueness to definition, from superstition to rationality; a progress which, steadily continuing throughout the whole century, reached a remarkable climax in the legislation of Edward I (1272–1307) in England, Philip the Fair (1285–1314) in France, and Alphonso the Wise (1252–84) in Castile.

Progress toward more rational thought is well illustrated in the fate of the ordeal. At the fourth Lateran council of 1215 Pope Innocent III, himself a canon lawyer of supreme distinction, condemned the ordeal as irrational and, for the future, forbade the clergy to attend and sanctify it.

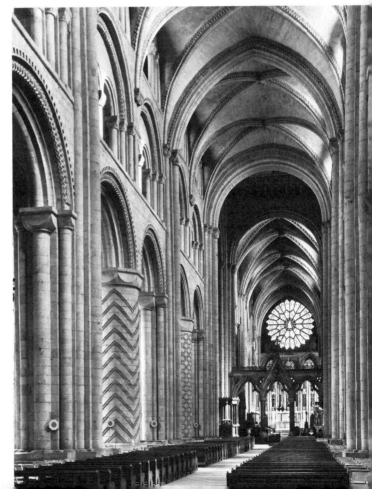

The Norman nave of Durham Cathedral, begun in 1093. (A. F. Kersting.)

Supernatural sanction thus withdrawn, the loss of the ordeal's sacred validity forced secular governments to devise substitutes for it. At first, they hardly knew where to turn to cope with this bewildering problem. Gradually, the English government filled this grievous judicial gap by asking those indicted to accept the verdict of a jury of their neighbors. In time, these groups developed into the modern petty jury.

All through the century the scope of European government was becoming wider, institutions and customs more precisely defined. Rulers insisted more and more upon responsibility and control of those who held positions of trust and power. King Louis IX (1226–70) and his successors in France carried out frequent enquiries into the country's administration, using first the friars and later lawyers as their commissioners. In England Henry III (1216–72) and his son Edward I (1272–1307), conducted investigation after investigation into the affairs of the countryside to preserve royal rights from attrition and to put down the perennial corruption that was everywhere the curse of both central and local government in the Middle Ages.

Governmental Change and Reform

The first series of reforms took place at the Exchequer—reforms devised by Henry III's Poitevin civil servants Peter des Roches and his nephew Peter de Rivaux, both of whom had been servants of King John. Peter de Rivaux was a great administrative brain, fertile with innovating schemes. For a short time in the early 1230s this comparatively obscure official gathered into his own hands so many offices and powers that he, and he alone, almost completely controlled both central and local government: powers which he then used to carry out a drastic overhaul of the royal financial system, extending the use of an improved system of tallies[1] (already introduced under King John) to speed up accounting procedures at the Exchequer, taking control of the royal estates in the counties out of the sheriffs' hands and placing them under the control of special officials. These new controls cut off the profits that the sheriffs had formerly retained for themselves at the government's expense and raised the normal revenues to a level high enough for the king to get along fairly well from year to year.

At the same time, the government began to refine and extend the judicial arrangements introduced by Henry II,[2] both in the central courts of

---

[1] Wooden sticks marked with notches representing the amount of a debt or payment. The stick was split lengthwise across the notches, the debtor and creditor each keeping one of the halves, the agreement, or tallying, of which constituted legal proof of the debt or payment.
[2] See pp. 81 ff.

justice and, with more effective devices for dealing with cases, locally. The separate records of the king's bench date from the year 1234, and the court began to hear appeals in civil cases from the earlier court of Common Pleas and other courts and handled cases in which the king's interests were in some way involved. At the highest level, justice and politics were always intermingled; considerations of royal favor and patronage always interfered, in what we should consider thoroughly illegitimate ways, with the judicial process. For a long time, therefore, the proceedings of the new court still mingled with the political and administrative actions of the royal council—until, at last, by the early years of Edward I's reign, it became a more or less separate institution. Likewise, more flexible institutions and procedures replaced the cumbersome Eyre. Early in the century the government appointed panels of local knights and gentlemen (generally four) to conduct assizes, or civil pleas, and at about the same time appointed similar groups to "deliver the gaols," that is, to try imprisoned suspects accused of crime. Very soon afterward, professional judges, sent out on circuit from Westminster, began to perform these functions, often sitting together with local

Salisbury Cathedral.
(J. Allan Cash—Rapho-
Guillumette.)

associates. Experimental arrangements gradually hardened into well-defined institutions, so that, once again by Edward I's early years, these local judicial sessions were regularly taking place, in some counties twice, thrice, and even four times a year, thus approaching the ideal which Magna Carta had stipulated for the petty assizes. Between 1285 and 1293 statutes formulated regular, definite arrangements for this localized administration of justice to institute the "assizes," more or less as they are known in England today: justices traveling the countryside on recognized circuits, deciding civil cases which litigants chose to initiate before them, others transferred from the central courts to be heard locally, and passing judgments upon a wide variety of criminal offenses. Later governments made some modifications in the system, but by the end of the fourteenth century it had settled down to twice yearly visitations of the counties with the circuits staffed by men of the highest legal qualifications.

Despite their immense advantages, all these reforms and innovations brought hardship to the minor nobility (or the gentry, as they have traditionally been called), for they required of this particular class extensive and unpaid service, as jurors, as coroners, and as local commissioners of many kinds. Moreover, the government now relied upon this class to provide the sheriffs. Out of twenty-five sheriffs in Cambridgeshire during the thirteenth century, nineteen were local gentry. With the increasing functions of government, these officials became very hardworked indeed, and the reforms at the Exchequer had cut out the possibility of their making a profit from their offices. Indeed, some of them now had to be paid a salary to induce them to serve at all, and after their term of office was over the Exchequer might hound them for years, even for decades, to pay arrears of dues for which they were held personally responsible but which they had been unable to collect. Any local administrative jobs (and they were more or less compulsory) cost time and money. And the jobs were many; the sheriff's was only the most prominent among them. Increasing self-government was being forced upon the upper classes, and they took to it only reluctantly. However desirable its long-term results may be, the extension of government always in its early stages provokes resentment, and at this time a considerable number of middling landowners and gentry was gaining a very bitter experience of local government.

Moreover, the narrowing of the class from which these administrators were drawn imposed ever greater burdens upon the rest. Legally, knights were required for administration, and the number of knights steadily diminished from about 5,000 in Henry I's day to a mere 1,200 by the beginning of Edward I's reign. Social change had transformed these knights from tough military adventurers with rich prospects of loot and booty—and even the grant of new estates when the king led a successful campaign on foreign territory—into hardworked civilian administrators. Prospects were so relatively unattractive that men were more and more reluctant to become knights and thus attract these local burdens unto themselves; so much so that from 1224 the government introduced a system of compulsion called "distraint of knighthood." Men of a certain income (from 1241 it was £20 a year) were forced to become knights or pay a heavy fine: more or less "conscript knights," most unwilling to accept the tasks imposed upon them. The English were learning self-government the hard way, and they resented it.

At a higher social level the magnates also found cause for resentment. As we have seen, Magna Carta imposed definite, even stringent, limitations upon the king, but it did not solve the problem of political discussion and participation. To use their own thirteenth-century terms, the Charter had, to some extent, solved the problem of *jurisdictio*, but it had left almost untouched the problem of *gubernaculum*. Royal exploitation of the vagueness of feudal law and feudal right had provoked resentment, and the Great Charter in 1215 had placed definite limitations on such exploitation. Thus, in the thirteenth century the way was left open for a transfer of interest from law to politics. After 1234 the rights and limitations imposed by the Charter were never really in doubt, but obviously the question of the *gubernaculum*, the problems involved in political discussions, could not be settled by a similar kind of legal limitation. Circumstances now called for a more revolutionary form of political control.

Henry III Versus the Magnates

When King John died, Henry III was a child only eight years old. The small group of magnates and officials, headed first by William the Marshal and later by Hubert de Burgh, who guided the affairs of the kingdom during Henry's minority, found it wise to obtain approval for their decisions from a general body of magnates meeting from time to time in common council—proceedings which both strengthened a genuine tradition of counsel by the great men of the realm in important matters and, more dubiously, created something of a new aristocratic vested interest in continuous political action at the highest level. When in 1227, at the age of nineteen, Henry announced the end of his official minority, following the custom of his ancestors he reverted to the practice of running affairs through an administrative council of *domesticii*, or officials. Soon one of the burning questions of the day became: Had he the right to rule exclusively through this type of council, or was he legally obliged, as many of the magnates claimed, to give them a predominant share in decision-making at the center of government as well as leaving them control of their own spheres of interest in the countryside? Henry firmly insisted on his exclusive right to choose his own counselors and servants. From the strictly traditional point of view, right was on his side, and even when the greatest of troubles overwhelmed him he would never surrender his theoretical claim to appoint his own counselors. Just as the general activities of government were being greatly extended during the thirty years of Henry's personal rule, his administrative council became steadily more professional: it included the chief officers of the realm and of the royal household, who at this time were not sharply distinguishable, and a little group of king's clerks, and others, honored by such designations as "counselor," "familiar," "special," or "secretary." In spite of progressively deteriorating relationships with the baronage, a few magnates always attended, including the Earl of Lincoln, and for several years even the future archrebel Simon de Montfort, himself (although, at times, both seem to have been as unpopular with the rest of the baronage as were the professional counselors). Moreover, contrary to what we should expect from vehement complaints from Henry's xenophobic opponents about excessive favor shown to foreigners, especially foreign royal relations, on the whole Henry chose Englishmen. During the 1250s the head of the council was, in fact, John Mansel, the humble son of a country priest, and his highest office was that of chancellor of the Exchequer.

Ecclesiastical elements were strong—abbots, a Templar, Franciscans, and Dominicans being amongst them. As so often happens in times of comparatively rapid change, strong vested interests detested the promotion of new types of men. The older religious orders, particularly the Benedictine Monks, hated and feared the popularity of the new orders of friars, and Matthew Paris, the brilliantly venomous chronicler of St. Albans, one of the richest Benedictine houses in the country, sneered that "in those days Friars Preachers[3] and Minorities[4] were made councillors and ambassadors of Kings. As once those who wore soft raiment were in King's houses so then the vilely clad were in the houses, chambers and palaces of princes."

On the other hand, to do Henry justice, he never made a direct, frontal attack upon the tradition of taking common counsel with the magnates. Nor, unfortunately, after a series of great and fruitful discussions during the years 1234–37, did he ever make any genuine effort to meet the views of the baronage and to secure their cooperation—an attitude of almost unbelievable insouciance, not to say folly, considering the social structure and practical distribution of power within the state at that time. After 1237, although the barons continued to give advice, they found, increasingly to their baffled frustration, that it was rarely taken. Even worse, they suspected that Henry was capable of criminal tactics to get his own way. As early as 1234 disastrous rumors spread that he had condoned the attempted assassination of Richard the Marshal in Ireland. Almost inevitably, inexorably, a developing bureaucratic regime (limited as it was by modern standards) clashed, often in highly irritating ways, with somewhat inert

[3] Dominicans.
[4] Franciscans.

traditional conventions. Institutions and government, generally, as suggested earlier, were now progressing from vagueness to increasing definition, and the old ill-defined obligation to give advice and an equally ill-defined right to be consulted had become difficult to reconcile with the growing pressures of executive government.

To add to his growing troubles, Henry alienated the clergy. During the 1240s and the 1250s an alliance between the king and the papacy to screw money from the English Church produced in its turn an alliance between some of the clergy and some of the baronage to resist such demands.

The Baronial Revolt

These chronic domestic suspicions, already heightened from time to time by acute quarrels between the king and his magnates, created a tension-ridden atmosphere ripe for head-on conflict: the great baronial movement of 1258. The immediate occasion of the baronial protest, however, sprang from a short-term crisis in foreign affairs. After the death of the Emperor Frederick II of Hohenstaufen in 1250, Pope Innocent IV (1243–54), attempting to eradicate the perpetual nightmare of the papacy (the encirclement of the Papal States by a German ruler who controlled Lombardy, Tuscany, southern Italy, and Sicily), offered the Sicilian crown to Henry's second son, Edmund. Henry accepted the offer, undertook to pay for the war, without which the plan would have been the merest of paper dreams, and soon found himself backing papal debts to the tune of 135,000 marks. Even worse, for an intensely pious man, he was under threat of excommunication if he failed to pay them.

Without consultation of any kind, Henry dashed headlong into these expensive foreign schemes: schemes which benefited only his family while leaving his unfortunate subjects to bear their heavy cost. Now in desperate straits for money, he was forced to turn to the baronage for assistance, only to meet a vigorous opposition led, amongst others, by his own brother-in-law, the Frenchman Simon de Montfort, now Earl of Leicester. The personal grievances of the magnates generally complicated, indeed often dominated, political quarrels during the Middle Ages, and, at this time, personal resentment against the king, the result of an involved dispute over his wife's dower, strongly reinforced de Montfort's unquestioned political idealism. A certain personal antipathy further compounded these involved relationships, for the king was once heard to say that although he was terrified of thunder he was even more terrified of Simon de Montfort.

Henry had hoped that an appeal to the baronage would bring support for the Sicilian venture and extricate him from his financial difficulties. He badly misjudged their temper, for, far from tamely approving his past actions, they determined to assist him only upon their own terms. They made possible a compromise settlement with the Pope, but, at the same time, in two Parliaments held during 1258 they forced the king to capitulate to a reform program which took the direction of affairs completely out of his hands. The barons insisted, in the Provisions of Oxford, that he hand over the day-to-day direction of affairs to a jointly chosen Council of Fifteen which, in turn, three times a year was subjected to political control by a "parliament"[5] of twelve chosen from the whole body of the baronage, though others might also attend if they so wished. Having for the moment, though only for the moment, solved the problem of political control, the new council went on to discuss very practical administrative reforms—to investigate the conduct of local officials and to send out a General Eyre to deal with the abuses and complaints which these investigations quickly brought to light. Sheriffs, in future, were to be local men of property appointed for one year only, and they were to be paid salaries. The councillors undertook to enforce the provisions of Magna Carta more effectively and directed that no government orders whatsoever were to be issued without their approval.

The commissioners of the General Eyre worked exceedingly hard for the next two years and such vigorous activity achieved considerable practical results. This, after all, was only carrying on, though perhaps rather more effectively than usual, one of the better traditions of Angevin government, including Henry's own, and a good deal of corruption in local government was, for the time, cleared up.

So far, proceedings within the ranks of the reformers had been fairly harmonious, though it would be mistaken to see, from the beginning, an entire people united in defiance of the king and his family. After all, Simon de Montfort was Henry's brother-in-law, and for a time (1259–60) even the Lord Edward, the heir to the throne, went over to the baronial movement. Soon, however, serious dissensions, divided the reformers. Men of the younger generation opposed their fathers, the clergy were divided amongst themselves, and in the greater towns, particularly in London, the lesser citizens took the opportunity to assail the dominance of the greater whom they regarded as their oppressors. The Welsh Marcher lords supported now one side, now the other.

Like many radical movements, that of 1258 flowed, almost of its own momentum, beyond the original intentions of many of its early adherents. Early in 1259 some of the more radical spirits demanded the extension of reform to baronial lands and liberties. Much of the regional government of the country lay, after all, in baronial hands. Baronial administration collectively affected at least as many people as the royal administration, and baronial officials were no less oppressive and corrupt than the king's. The

---

[5] For the contemporary meaning of this term, see p. 147.

idea of an extension of reforms which so vitally touched their own interests was anything but appealing to the more conservative members of the baronage. Such radical reactionaries claimed that the administration of their lands and liberties was an entirely private matter—in view of their own recent actions a thoroughly illogical, out-of-date claim. If they had arrogated unto themselves the right to intervene in those affairs of the king which touched the public interest, similar activities of their own could hardly be denied the same intensive scrutiny.

Their point of view had, in fact, been out-of-date for some time, for Henry's own government had been enquiring into the conduct of liberties and franchises.[6] Once more, matters became immensely complicated by personal issues and personal problems. Richard de Clare, the powerful Earl of Gloucester, took the conservative side, while de Montfort led the new radicals. In spite of divisions, the lands of the magnates were brought under the Eyre and under the justices in March of 1259. The following October, the council issued the Provisions of Westminster, a code which brought together the reforming decisions and the legal and administrative changes of the previous eighteen months and also alleviated some of the grievances of the lesser gentry. For example, they gave tenants better protection than they had ever before enjoyed against abuses by landlords.

In spite of continued divisions between 1259 and 1261, the baronial council consolidated its hold over both central and local government. Continued reform brought a new note of optimism into English life. A St. Albans writer, generally somewhat given to dwelling upon the black side of things, summed up the gains and losses of these times by remarking that, notwithstanding the devastating weather and a meager harvest, "England, which had long suffered the injuries and tyrannies as it were, of many Kings, in this year began to breathe with long-desired reforms and a new spirit of justice arose within her."

This happy state of affairs was not to continue. Apart from the fact that many of the barons resented the extension of the reforms to their own lands, they had no particular longing for a permanent change in the processes of government. King Henry naturally wished to revert to what he regarded as normal rule. Many men—Richard de Clare and others—had accepted the Provisions of Oxford as an emergency measure. Insofar as the General Eyre had instituted better justice and the Provisions of Oxford had brought legal and administrative reforms, the baronial government to de Clare and those of like mind seemed to have done its work, and the time had arrived for a restoration of more normal conditions. Others, led by Simon de Montfort, were determined to make the Provisions of Oxford the permanent basis of the government of the kingdom.

In 1260 and 1261, during a very complicated and prolonged series of

[6] For franchises, see pp. 83, 143.

disputes, many barons went over to support the King—as did the Lord Edward—and a new "royal" party consolidated around the heir to the throne. In 1261 the Pope absolved the king from his oath to maintain the Provisions. For the next two years stalemate, an uneasy peace, prevailed between the two opposing groups of magnates. Then, as relations again worsened, a final attempt to avoid disaster by submitting the quarrel to the arbitration of St. Louis of France failed when, in the Mise of Amiens (1264), he exceeded his commission by restoring to Henry the right of complete control over his own council. The baronial movement for reform at last became a baronial revolt: De Montfort, taking to arms, shattered the royal forces at the battle of Lewes (1264).

Though they were steeped in the tradition of 1215, the barons in 1258 had successfully evolved institutions very much in advance of the crude methods of control set out in Clause 61 of Magna Carta. They no longer left the executive in the king's hands, holding over his head the threat of armed force in case of his recalcitrance. Through the Council of Fifteen, they controlled the executive to so great a degree that they had, in a new and revolutionary way, put the powers of the Crown into commission. At the same time, they accepted the bureaucratic developments of the previous half-century; exposing serious defects in the law and administration, they cooperated with trained legists to draft and promulgate extensive reforms. Yet administration, even the people running it, continued in much the same way during the years of crisis and experiment. John Mansel continued in government as an influential member of the Council of Fifteen. New minds and new methods at the summit, as so often in revolutions, more fully and in a fresh spirit controlled and extended existing administrative machinery.

Yet, in spite of this success, the split in the baronial ranks and the horror (to many contemporary minds) of levying war upon the king meant the inevitable collapse of baronial control. His Pyrrhic victory at Lewes left Simon de Montfort in an almost impossibly isolated position. Massive defections left united baronial government no longer possible, forcing him to rule through a narrow oligarchy supported by a premature attempt to bring the middling ranks of society more fully into political life. In 1264 he summoned knights of the shire to Parliament, and the following year, for the first time, representatives from the towns. Unfortunately for him, his quite genuine attempts to broaden the basis of governmental support bore, in the conditions of the day, one fatal flaw: they ignored the king and they ignored too many of the kingdom's great and powerful men. Civil war broke out again, and in 1265 de Montfort was defeated and killed at the battle of Evesham.

After de Montfort's death it took another two years for the royal forces to subdue the last of the rebels. Although Henry III declared that his royal powers were unaffected by the crisis which had begun in 1258, many of the practical reforms which the baronial movement had achieved were reaffirmed in the Statute of Marlborough (1267) and thus became part of the permanent law of the land.

Edward I: Reform and War

Edward I, Henry's son, who succeeded him in 1272, as a former, though short-lived, ally of de Montfort, recognized the need to continue this policy of stabilizing the gains of the reform movement and the need to carry reform still further: to remove, or at least to reduce as much as possible, the perennial anomalies and abuses the feudal world, whose system of government was deeply rooted in property rights, perpetually generated. This early policy of stabilization unfortunately changed in his later years into a harsh program of exploitation to finance his own feudal ambitions in Wales, Scotland, and Flanders.

Edward was a highly competent but quite conventional man, working to make the most of his resources. He was also, unfortunately, overambitious in his schemes of feudal conquest. Treacherous and violent in temper —quite prepared to break the most solemn promises when he considered them to have been forced upon him and capable of the most appalling exhibitions of rage. On one occasion, in front of the whole court, he tore by the handful the hair from the head of the unfortunate Prince of Wales.

The Statute of Marlborough, besides consolidating the reforms of Henry III's reign, became the basis for new legislation which marks Edward's earlier years, some of which dealt rather more effectively with similar matters. Renewed efforts were still needed, for the full effects of administrative reform rarely lasted for long under medieval conditions. Following the civil war, abuses had again seeped back into local government. The new reforms had, in large measure, to be of a conservative kind, for, although the king himself led the way, they had to be carried through with the consent and cooperation of the magnates. Edward always emphasized the personal character of the monarchy, yet, at the same time, he restored to the aristocracy their traditional place in government: they once again gave counsel and the king accepted it, but they never dominated the *council*.

The reforming period of Edward's reign fell between 1274 and 1290: during those years the relations between the king and baronage were harmonious. As Edward stated in the statutes of these years, he issued them "with the counsel of the prelates, earls and other faithful men of the Kingdom," "at the instance of the magnates," "for the betterment of his Kingdom and fuller administration of justice as is demanded by the kingly office," to remedy many omissions and defects in the law.[7]

[7] Preambles to Edwardian Statutes, in W. Stubbs, *Select Charters*, ed. H. W. C. Davis (9th ed.; Oxford, 1921), pp. 451, 473.

Edward's first actions when he returned home from a crusade in 1274 show how quickly the standards of local government had deteriorated. He immediately ordered an enquiry into abuses, and the results were compiled by March 1275 into the famous Hundred Rolls, which then formed the basic material for a widespread program of reform. The king severely punished numerous offenders and embarked on a comprehensive program of legislation which continued over the next fifteen years. In 1275, and again a decade later, statutes dealt with the old perennial questions, so often heard of before, of abuses committed by sheriffs, bailiffs, and other local officials. Other statutes attempted to rationalize procedure at the Exchequer to prevent officials from defrauding the king and exploiting his subjects. Edward also codified the system of local police organization, such as it was. No completely new pattern or system of local government came out of all this. Edward used all the existing institutions, trying, not entirely successfully, to restore efficiency and standards of honesty at all levels of the governmental system: in local government, in the Wardrobe,[8] in the Exchequer, in the Chancery, he made a determined attempt to impose greater rectitude and efficiency.

The magnates and other landowners welcomed revision of the feudal system of land tenure and its various controls. Although feudalism was now dead as a military system—by 1300 the feudal summons produced no more than 375 knights for the royal armies—it remained socially as vital as ever, for feudal forms continued for centuries as the basis of all land tenures. Owing to subinfeudation[9] and gifts to the Church, lords had been losing control of their assets. The disaster of subinfeudation was that if the tenants of a great lord (or any other lord for that matter) sold their lands, the buyers held such estates in fee from the sellers, not from the original lord who, therefore, lost his valuable rights of escheat, marriage, and wardship. The same losses occurred when churches acquired lands, for churches, being undying corporations, produced no heirs to be in wardship, to pay reliefs, or to be married, and they offered no possibility of escheats. In both cases, lords lost potentially valuable revenues. The statutes of *Quia Emptores* (1290) and Mortmain (1279) put an end to these obvious abuses, for they required purchasers of estates to become the legal feudal tenants of the original lords and forbade alienations to churches without a royal license. Other statutes gave lords a more secure control over lands which they alienated for short periods or for special purposes and gave them much firmer powers of discipline over their estate officials. New legislation thus prevented, for the future, the legal attrition of estates and restored a firmer control over their property to both the king and the feudal classes.

[8] A department of the royal household which was also extremely important in national finance since it dealt with raising loans and with military expenditure.
[9] See p. 68.

Other legislation, mainly in the royal interest, pleased the feudal classes far less. Most magnates, and many lesser men, exercised franchisal jurisdiction. Justice over any crime infringing the king's peace was franchisal, and in the conditions of the day the delegation of these rights or some of them was an almost essential form of decentralization. Powerful men treasured and jealously guarded such franchises for the sake of revenue, prestige, and power. To make their possession more secure, they tended to claim that such rights were feudal in origin, that is, that they held them in the same way that they held estates, or claimed them as appurtenant to land so that they could be bought or sold with it. Kings, on the other hand, claimed that these franchises were regalian; in other words, that they derived exclusively from royal grants. Difficulties arose, however, because many men whose ancestors had exercised such powers from time immemorial could produce no written royal grant or charter in support of their claims. Henry III and Edward I increasingly denied the independence of the franchise holders and more and more stressed their responsibility to the Crown and to the community. Apart from the Crown's need to preserve its powers, the practical reasons for such a policy are obvious enough. A very common franchise, for example, was the private hundred: in 1274 no less than 358 out of 628 hundreds were in private hands. As the hundred was the basic subunit of the shire for the administration of justice, inefficiently run private hundreds could easily become safe refuges for criminals and a danger to the neighboring countryside. In 1278 the Statute of Gloucester instructed the justices to investigate titles to franchises—an instruction which the franchise-holders fiercely resented.

In recent years scholars have increasingly turned from study of legislation to study of the subsequent administration upon which its success depends. Except for Edward's feudal land legislation, a much less happy picture now emerges than in the days when historians drew their conclusions almost entirely from the peremptory words of the statutes. The king was, from 1276, much occupied by affairs in Wales, but even without this distracting burden it seems that his varied programs initiated far more than the administrators at his command could complete. The contemporary *Annals of Dunstable* even state that no good at all came out of the great enquiry of 1274. Although the author exaggerated, his words were not entirely without foundation, for the judges who dealt with the wrongs which the enquiry revealed moved far too slowly to satisfy the victims of injustice or to be very disturbing to the corrupt.[10] As late as 1287 the justices were still dealing with cases uncovered thirteen years before. Another great inquest, begun in 1279, concerning lands and tenements over the whole country might well have produced another Domesday Book, but no action was ever taken on the results and it may never have been

[10] F. M. Powicke, *The Thirteenth Century* (Oxford, 1953), p. 360.

completed. The 1285 Statute of Winchester, in the end, did very little to improve public order. Even the *Quo Warranto*[11] enquiries into the franchises which Edward pushed forward in the teeth of great opposition were, in most counties, less extensive than he had planned, and his struggle against the franchise-holders ended with a compromise in a statute of 1290 and subsequent interpretation of it by the judges. The campaign did something to preserve royal rights, far less to improve the quality of justice in the franchises. Edward's ambitious plans were too much for the slender administrative resources of the day: "There were too many projects and too few responsible heads."[12]

Intense corruption exacerbated inadequacy. High standards of rectitude in administration are a comparatively recent development. Even in days when the public normally expected officials to make considerable fortunes out of the public service, Edward's administrators continually overstepped even low thresholds of decency. Edward sternly punished Adam de Stratton, his Exchequer clerk and Master of the Works, for corruption in 1278 and again in 1290–92. On this last occasion royal servants who carried out a search found no less than £12,666.17.7 in cash in Adam's house—and this in an age when gentlemen thought an income of £20 a year prosperity! Between 1289 and 1293 some of the judges and many other officials were put on trial for corruption, and the king's commissioners investigated between 600 and 700 cases of official malpractice. In spite of all this, it is doubtful whether standards improved very much during the king's later years. At the beginning of the next reign, Walter Langton, his treasurer from 1295 to 1307, was accused, among other things, of adultery, murder, simony, doing homage to the devil, intimidation of sheriffs and juries, wrongful imprisonment, and cheating the king of his revenues. He probably made an even greater fortune than Adam de Stratton; at his fall, it may have amounted to £20,000, as well as a large landed estate. Yet, even after these spectacular revelations, Edward II took him back into favor.

From 1290 onward, two decades of more or less continuous warfare or preparations for warfare—war in Wales, in Scotland, in Flanders—shattered Edward's earlier cooperation with the magnates, leaving him faced with insoluble problems. Maintaining and financing his armies placed too great a strain on the slender resources of personal monarchy and drove the king to demand from his subjects far greater sums of money than they were willingly prepared to give.

These wars were the first major test of the military machine since the loss of Normandy under King John, and in the eighty or so years since 1205 conditions had changed to the king's disadvantage. The decline of

---

[11] The opening words of the writ *Quo Warranto* ordering enquires "by what warrant" franchises were held.

[12] D. W. Sutherland, *Quo Warranto Proceeedings in the Reign of Edward I, 1278–1294* (Oxford, 1963), p. 186.

military feudalism had made it far more difficult to raise an army.[13] To do so, Edward resorted (amongst other means) to coercion. In 1297 he commanded all men with incomes of £20 a year and more to assemble in London for military service overseas. Far from bringing forth men, the command generated a spirit of violent opposition. Moreover, the technical demands of warfare had vastly changed from those of earlier times. The backbone of the army was no longer mounted men in heavy armor, but archers, light cavalry, and infantry, now provided largely by the expansion of the royal household forces with the addition of Welsh mercenaries and men recruited under contract by the magnates. Unlike the feudal levy, the king had to pay this new type of contract army out of the royal coffers.

Though by modern standards these forces were small, almost minute,[14] their cost shattered the royal finances. Until 1290 Edward had enjoyed considerable financial success. After the organization of a customs system in 1275, he received about £13,000 a year from taxes on trade—an addition to his income of about 30 percent. He could add to it, from time to time, subsidies on movable goods.[15] Between 1290 and 1307 he took no less than seven of these subsidies, and all of them were levied at a very high rate. The "tenth"[16] of 1291 alone brought in £116,000—an unprecedented sum for medieval England. His average annual revenue from this source was probably about £30,000. All this amounted to an organizational and financial revolution, but even so the sums gathered were totally inadequate for a long period of warfare.

If Edward's earlier reform program had overtaxed his servants, the warlike ambitions of his later years crashed into financial and administrative breakdown, bringing in their train dangerous political resentments and tensions. Between 1290 and 1297 resistance and evasion reduced the yield of the subsidy by at least 50 percent, and the royal debts became so desperate that by the end of his reign Edward owed money everywhere—to Italian bankers, to magnates and ministers, to courtiers and officials. The humbler members of his household were even in arrears for their wages, robes, and shoes. He left his son financial and political bankruptcy.

The Development of Parliament

Edward I, although enormously talented, was cast in the conventional mold of his generation, directing and cooperating with the landed classes in the government of the realm and relentlessly pressing hereditary feudal claims to territory in the same way and in the same spirit that contemporary

---

[13] See pp. 86–88 on the decline of the feudal host.
[14] The army that Edward led in North Wales in 1277 consisted of 800 knights, 15,000 footmen, and 370 archers and crossbowmen.
[15] A kind of capital levy on the value of men's personal property.
[16] A tax of a tenth of the value of a man's movable goods, as distinct from his property in lands and buildings.

barons pressed feudal claims to family inheritances. Although he is now remembered as the most prominent of medieval English legislators, he himself probably regarded his legislation and the more developed institutions which it produced less as ends in themselves than as mere expedients, the ways and means of supporting martial ambitions and territorial conquests—his conquest of Wales, his attempted subjugation of Scotland, and his campaigns in Flanders. The most prominent and the most enduring of

Artist's conception of Edward I's Parliament of 1295: The king is flanked by Alexander of Scotland, Llewellyn of Wales, archbishops, lords, and others. From Wriothesley manuscript in the Royal Library, Windsor. Drawing done by a herold for Thomas Wriothesley, Garter King-of-Arms, 1505–34. (The New York Public Library Picture Collection.)

these expedients, one so far only incidentally mentioned, was the development of Parliament during his reign.

To understand the meaning of Parliament at this time, it is best to forget completely its modern composition, organization, and functions. It has become something of a commonplace with historians of institutions that their form and functions often become quite different from those of their early days. The very word "parliament" was originally something of a slang term in medieval French (the language of the English aristocracy in the thirteenth century), and it meant any kind of discussion. Towns assembled for parliaments, or magnates could hold them for their tenants, especially their borough tenants. The French chronicler Joinville describes how King Louis IX of France and his young wife, to avoid the jealousy of his formidable mother Queen Blanche, met secretly beneath a privy stair in the palace of Pontoise and there they "held their parliament." Only gradually was the word restricted to the greatest and the most prominent public assembly of the realm.

The English Parliament was not in origin exclusively a political institution. It was also a law court, a royal administrative device rather than a popular assembly, a more efficent method of extending a tighter hold over the country's administration and for dealing out more effective justice. There were always legal disputes of exceptional complication and difficulty which particular courts felt to be beyond their competence. Therefore, from the 1240s, possibly earlier, judges began to postpone difficult cases to the law terms when they could be discussed with all their colleagues together with members of the royal council. Such interdepartmental discussions, which contemporary records called "parliaments," took place three or four times a year. As time went on litigants began to take the opportunity of these meetings to petition the king for justice. In February 1305, for example, 480 discontented people handed in petitions when Parliament assembled.

From about 1252 we can trace a tendency for these judicial-*cum*-administrative sessions to coincide in time and place with political assemblies. In spite of the great dramatic clashes between king and barons, the normal, and essential, condition of political life was cooperation between them, and from time to time the great men of the realm met the king in council for discussions—discussions which were also designated "parliaments."

At first, representatives (from the fifteenth century onward called the House of Commons), nowadays the most prominent people in such assemblies, took a very humble third place after the lay and ecclesiastical magnates and the judges and other royal servants. The great jurist Bracton (d. 1268) analyzed political life in terms which completely ignored representatives:

> The King has a superior, namely God, as also the law by which he is made King, and his court, to wit, the earls and barons. And, therefore, if the

King is unbridled, that is without the law, they ought to put a bridle upon him, unless they themselves are unbridled together with the King. And in that case the subject people will cry out and say, "Lord Jesus, with bit and bridle bind fast their jaws.

Representatives were summoned for various reasons throughout the thirteenth century, but examples from before 1250 are so disjointed that it is quite impossible to draw any firm conclusions from them. From this time onward, however, two considerations seem to have forced on the growth of representation: the need for wider political support and the need for taxation.

Under Edward I financial considerations (the need, already discussed, to meet the cost of his aggressive policies) may well have been more vital than political needs. It was a well-established principle, firmly enshrined in Magna Carta, that the king might take money from his subjects only with their consent. In his early years Henry III resorted to traveling around the countryside negotiating for money with rich individuals, religious communities, and boroughs. What could be more natural, to save time and effort, than to substitute a single collective agreement for these multifarious haggles? Henry summoned representatives from the shires in 1254 to consent to taxation. Acting upon a precedent of 1268, Edward I and his advisers, between 1283 and 1297, developed in the writ of summons a formula which legally bound the communities of the shires and the boroughs to act on the promises which representatives made in their name. This ingenious legal device (derived from Roman law) was most important for the firm development of Parliament as an institution. By making local repudiation of parliamentary grants legally impossible, the writ ensured that parliamentary procedure served royal financial needs. In some European countries which failed to establish this vital working principle, the local communities remained free to repudiate the financial promises which their representatives made, and parliaments ceased to exist because kings found it financially useless to go on calling them together.

As to politics, in 1265 Simon de Montfort, anxious to gain wider support, summoned representatives from both shires and boroughs. Although Edward I always summoned representatives when he intended to demand taxation, and sometimes when he did not, he still did not regard representatives as an essential part of such an assembly.[17] In 1300 a meeting of magnates and royal servants without representatives could still be called a Parliament. It took another period of acute political tension, the reign of Edward II (1307–27), to establish them firmly as an essential part of the institution. Then both the king and his magnate opponents, each appealing for support against the other, called the Commons more and

---

[17] Out of fifty-seven Parliaments between 1272 and 1307, only sixteen contained representatives of various kinds. There were, in addition, another twelve assemblies (also without representatives) which some modern authorities class as Parliaments, though they are only called councils in contemporary sources.

more frequently to their councils until the habit hardened into custom and custom into law.

The English Parliament was thus a distinctly composite institution. In the last decade of the thirteenth century the legal writer Fleta could still describe it almost exclusively in terms of a court: "The King holds his court in his council in his parliaments in the presence of the prelates, earls, barons, notables and others . . . where new remedies are found for new wrongs and justice is done to each man according to his deserts."[18] This judicial aspect of Parliament's activities may indeed have appeared to many, if not the majority, as its essential function. Considering the need for taxation and for political discussion with the great men, however, the king and his advisers thought in less exclusive terms, for as early as 1280 Edward I commanded a reorganization of the methods of Parliament, ordering a good deal of the growing judicial business, whose magnitude threatened to overwhelm its sessions, back into the lower courts "so that the King and his council can, without charge of other business, hear the great business of the realm and of foreign lands."[19] Moreover, after 1285 the timetable of its meetings, which (since the late 1240s, with some interruptions) had been almost as regular as those of other courts, began to break down. After 1290 there was no regular sequence of meetings, and the contemporary *Mirror of Justices* complained that Parliaments were being held only as and where the king willed instead of twice a year in London, that their business consisted of the taking of aids and the gathering of treasure to the neglect of justice.

Parliament was thus both a court, a judicial body, and a political assembly to deal with the state of the Kingdom, but these dual functions came to be at odds with each other, with the result that, in the course of the fourteenth century, its judicial work progressively declined and it became the predominantly political assembly which we know today. Its future development and its success, nevertheless, lay in a combination of functions: it became a vehicle of both exploitation and resistance—exploitation by the king who demanded money; resistance by representatives of the local communities who strongly objected to giving and often demanded concessions in return. If Parliament had served the interests of only one side, its life would have been short. It endured and flourished because both sides found it convenient to concentrate their efforts of demand and resistance in one body—a concentration which, in the end, enabled it to function successfully as a constructive organ of government and as the great guardian first of individual liberties, then of liberty[20] itself, and, centuries later, of democracy and the welfare state.

[18] Close Roll, 8 Edward I, n.6, dorse, quoted in W. Stubbs, *The Constitutional History of England in Its Origin and Development*, II (3rd ed.; Oxford, 1887), 276, n. 2.
[19] *Ibid.*
[20] "Liberty" originally meant a franchise, special privilege, or exemption from ordinary law. Its abstract meaning appeared only toward the end of the fifteenth century.

CHAPTER EIGHT

Edward I's early political success had been very much a personal tour de force. By 1307 the strains which the overambitious policies of his later years produced so greatly overshadowed his achievements that the magnates were seething with resentment. Edward II (1307–27), temperamentally unsuited to the exacting role of personal monarchy, might well have failed to make an effective ruler in even the most favorable circumstances. Worse still, because of his father's stubborn folly in refusing to allow him any part in state affairs, he was also the first king since the Norman Conquest totally untrained for his position. He began to reign with almost every card stacked against him.

Opposition broke out almost immediately, led by the king's ambitious, unpleasant, and not overcompetent cousin, Thomas, Earl of Lancaster. Although the great officials carried on a reforming tradition in administration, issuing excellent new regulations for the conduct of the royal household and the Exchequer, Thomas and his aristocratic allies waged civil war on the king. In 1322 Edward defeated and executed the earl, but failing to learn from experience once more so outraged aristocratic opinion that within five years another coalition of magnates deposed and murdered him, replacing him with his fifteen-year-old son, Edward III (1327–77).

The Later
Middle Ages

Edward III:
The Hundred Years War

Edward III's reign was comparatively free from internal strife, except for a series of incidents at the beginning of the Hundred Years War between 1339 and 1341, when, like his grandfather in his later years, he sometimes took important decisions without due cooperation with the magnates, decisions which, once again as in Edward I's day, badly overstrained the resources of the royal treasury.

By the end of this early crisis, however, Edward had grasped the conditions of political success, and from then onward lived in harmony with the powerful classes who really counted in the politics of the land. Unlike his father who was given to such unconventional hobbies as carpentry, thatching, and rowing—peasant occupations which drew down upon him the contempt of his own courtiers—Edward III shared to the full the conventional tastes and pleasures of the aristocracy. Social harmony contributed to political harmony. Edward was a superb general, and he may well have owed this new cooperation in large measure to his successful leadership of the nobility and gentry in the Hundred Years War against

France, from which some of them profited immensely, if somewhat sporadically, in the way of loot and ransoms.

With all the advantages of historical hindsight, we can also surmise that Edward's success was due as much to fortuitous circumstances as to his own abilities. France was far bigger, far more populous, far richer than England, and at first sight it would seem impossible that England could successfully wage war upon her over a long period. Edward was lucky, for his own country had reached a stage of economic development when the demand for English raw wool—an absolute necessity for the looms of Flanders and Italy—was at its peak. The Edwardian phases of the Hundred Years War coincided with the period just before the vast expansion of the English woolen cloth industry. The government could, therefore, tax wool very heavily indeed to pay for the war without ruining the export trade, thus avoiding the intense political resentment which a war mostly paid for out

Edward II, head of effigy in Gloucester Cathedral, *c.* 1331. (Helmut Gernsheim.)

of heavy direct taxation would certainly have aroused. Medieval men always looked upon direct taxes as an abnormal expedient rather than an annual burden, and warlike sentiment would hardly have survived for long under the pressure of regular demands for money—except, of course, among the nobility, and those sections of the gentry and the merchants who grew fat on war profits.

The war began in the chronic difficulties of the feudal relationship between the two kings (the King of England held Gascony as a fief of France) and from the assistance which the French gave the Scots against the English claim to the feudal overlordship of that kingdom. The first climax of English success came in 1346 with the great victory of Crécy and the capture of Calais, which became an important center of English trade until the French re-took it in 1558. The disaster of the Black Death

Wilton Diptych. *Left panel:* St. Edmund the King, St. Edward the Confessor, St. John the Baptist, and Richard II (kneeling). *Right panel:* Madonna and Child with angels wearing Richard's badge of the White Hart. (National Gallery, London.)

prevented a French *révanche*, making campaigns impossible for the next few years. French fortunes reached their nadir with their defeat at the hands of the Black Prince at Poitiers (1356), but from the mid-1360s the French made fairly steady progress against the English positions until, by 1380, little remained of Edward's conquest but Calais, Cherbourg, Bordeaux, and Bayonne.

From the end of the 1360s a period of renewed political difficulties set in. French successes meant the end of war profits. The king became prematurely senile and lost his grip upon affairs. Unfortunately, this was the beginning of long decades of weak government in England, which nobody alive at the time could possibly have prophesied. As Professor J. E. A. Joliffe has remarked,[1] owing to the uncontrollable accidents of birth and death (always the major flaw in a hereditary system of government) from 1370 to 1461, no really strong-willed and competent king occupied the throne for more than a few years together: a disastrous misfortune, for under medieval conditions the character of the monarch was always the key to political tranquility.

Richard II

Various noble factions competed for power during Edward's declining years and during the minority of his grandson, Richard II (1377–99), who was only ten years old when he came to the throne. These factions were both selfish and drearily incompetent, and in the heavy and politically disastrous poll taxes of 1379 and 1380 they imposed upon a discontented peasantry the last burden which provoked the great revolt of 1381. The factions tried to prolong their power beyond the period Richard rightly thought to be the natural term of a royal minority. His reaction to their domination was, however, rash in the extreme, uniting a tactlessly explicit theory of despotism—of "regality" as contemporaries called it—with practical, legal measures which seemed to threaten the security of property—and fear for the security of family property was the most bitter, the most intense emotion Richard could possibly have aroused in a land-conscious, agrarian community. Practical measures such as forced loans, compelling men to purchase pardons for earlier offenses which they had assumed to be forgiven and forgotten, and a demand for sealed "blank charters," so called because the king had *carte blanche* to insert conditions in them at a later date, terrified and alienated large numbers who originally had little direct interest in Richard's quarrels with the magnates. When, on the death of John of Gaunt, Duke of Lancaster, the richest man in England,

[1] *The Constitutional History of Medieval England* (3rd ed.; London, 1954), p. 473.

the king put his dubious principles into practice by disinheriting John's son, Henry, it seemed that no man in England would, in future, be safe from Richard's imperious designs. Henry, then in exile, returned to England, ostensibly to recover the duchy of Lancaster, his hereditary property, but ended, with a mixture of force and chicanery, by seizing the throne. Richard II shortly afterward died in Pontefract Castle, probably murdered.

The Lancastrian Kings and the Wars of the Roses

Henry IV's (1399–1413) fourteen-year reign was full of troubles, harassed as he was in his first seven years as king by disloyal magnates, rebellion in Wales, invasion from Scotland, and coastal raids by the French. Even when he had overcome these multifarious dangers, his peace was threatened by the factious ambitions of his own heir, the future Henry V, a vigorous son, impatiently, almost indecently, avid to take over power from an ailing father.

With Henry V (1413–22) at last there came calmer days. Henry renewed the Hundred Years War, determined to conquer the whole of France, which, according to the rules of feudal tenure, he could, with some surface plausibility, claim as his own rightful inheritance. After his victory at Agincourt in 1415, nothing more was heard of the aristocratic discontent and faction fighting which had so disturbed his father's reign and that of Richard II. The French war helped to bring about a new unity between king and barons. Unfortunately, Henry, like most of his family, had very little financial sense and renewed the ambitions of his great-grandfather, Edward III, without his great-grandfather's financial resources. With the rapid decline of raw wool exports, the yield of the customs had shrunk by nearly 45 percent since the middle of the fourteenth century. Henry V, therefore, had to raise so much money by direct taxation that the war rapidly lost its early popularity among most of the English. Adam of Usk, writing during Henry's last year on the throne, vehemently denounced the king for "rending every man throughout the Kingdom" to raise yet more money for his campaigns, men who paid "with murmurs and with smothered curses . . . from hatred of the burden."

Successful warfare called for a favorable combination of circumstances: a king who was a brilliant military leader, an enthusiastic aristocracy, and a populace prepared to contribute the necessary money. Henry V's premature death (he was only thirty-five) shattered this essential combination. The flow of his subjects' money was already drying up. Within a few years, the greater part of the aristocracy lost their enthusiasm for warfare, and his heir, Henry VI (1422–61), came to the throne a child but a few months old: a child who developed into a gentle, religiously minded, almost saintly adult, with most of the passive virtues that would have graced the life of a monk but entirely lacking the tough, decisive force which the kingly role demanded.

In spite of his genius, Henry V owed not a little of his success to the internal disunity and bitter political quarrels of the French higher nobility. As the French king, Charles VII (1422–61), reconciled the dissident factions and recovered strength, he gradually, but inexorably, recovered territory from the English, until in 1449–50, in a mopping-up operation which lasted a mere sixteen weeks, he drove their weak and disunited garrisons out of Normandy. Three years later he took over the remains of the English territory in Gascony.

Within two years, with the first battle of St. Albans (1455), the Wars of the Roses had begun in England—a war that continued, with long intervals of peace between comparatively short spells of fighting, until 1487. A French chronicler explained this near coincidence by saying that the English aristocracy had become so accustomed to fighting and looting that when they could no longer do so in France they turned and rent each other in England. This statement, although it has been endlessly repeated, has little to recommend it. For many years the English garrisons in France had been very small in numbers, too small, when they fled to England, to have any significant effect on domestic politics. Contemporary authors, when they mentioned them at all, wrote of pitiful, destitute refugees— objects of charity, not desperate, politically adventurous thugs.

Although failure in France gave critics plausible excuses for attacking the government at home, a more credible explanation for the political collapse of the mid-1450s lies in the character of Henry VI. His very virtues left him so feeble a ruler that he allowed his courtiers and officials to plunder his revenues, thus destroying his reputation with the Commons, for he was forced to ask them to make good the resulting financial deficit. Then, too, he allowed himself to become so blatantly dominated by one particular faction, led by William de la Pole, Duke of Suffolk, that confidence between the king and the nobility as a whole, so essential to government, declined almost to breaking point. Henry failed to fulfill the major royal function of standing above the nobility, keeping the peace between them so that they in turn maintained order and discipline in the countryside. It is hardly surprising that a section of the aristocracy ultimately attacked the king. It is perhaps more surprising that the majority of them remained loyal to him for so long.

The Yorkists and Henry VII

The house of York, like that of Lancaster, was descended from Edward III. Although the law of succession was confused and ambiguous, it could be,

John, Duke of Bedford (Henry V's brother), kneeling before St. George. From the *Bedford Book of Hours, c.* 1423. (Add. MS. 18850 f. 256b. Courtesy of the British Museum.)

and it was, argued that the Yorkists possessed a better title to the throne than the Lancastrians. Henry VI's political failure gave Richard, Duke of York, the opportunity to call in question the Lancastrian usurpation of the throne in 1399 and all its consequences and to put forward his own claims. Although on several occasions he failed to realize his ambitions, either by armed force or by negotiation, his son, Edward IV (1461–83), with the support of a tiny faction of nobles, seized the throne in 1461 during one of the acute phases of the civil war.

Edward's accession marked the turn of the tide politically, although the Yorkist dynasty ultimately failed to establish itself for, on his premature death, at the early age of forty-one, his younger brother, Richard of Gloucester, dethroned and probably murdered the fourteen-year-old heir, Edward V. Richard's actions roused such horror—rumor so blackened his character that he was even forced to deny publicly in the city of London reports that he had poisoned his queen—that only nine peers fought to defend his throne in 1485. Nor was enthusiasm for his opponent, Henry VII (1485–1509), at all widespread. Not more than 24,000 men, possibly as few as 18,000, fought in the battle of Bosworth which gave the throne to the Tudors, and probably few men alive at the time would have risked the suggestion that this small-scale conflict on a midland plain had finally decided the dynastic issue.

Although historians have traditionally regarded 1485 with its concomitant change of dynasty as a great dividing line in English history, a division between medieval England and the beginnings of modern England, there is really nothing to be said in favor of this theory. Despite the fact that the battle of Bosworth established a new dynasty that was to endure for over a century, the years from 1461 to 1509 present a remarkable unity in the style and activities of government. The end of the Hundred Years War in 1453 removed the major drain on the royal finances and, thus, one of the principal weaknesses of English monarchy. First Edward IV, then Henry VII, both determined, strong-willed, and decidedly conventional men, gained the loyalty (or at least the acquiescence) of the aristocracy through a discreet exercise of patronage. Both kings overwhelmed the recalcitrant minority with acts of attainder,[2] and in Henry VII's case with the imposition of heavy fines.[3] Keeping themselves, as far as possible, above the intrigues of particular factions of the nobility, they restored the traditional political unity of the propertied classes around their thrones; so much so that even the notorious Warwick the Kingmaker, Edward's most powerful and disgruntled opponent, found very little support among the nobility for his rebellions. Both kings made strenuous efforts to reduce disorder

[2] Acts of Parliament that, without trial, convicted offenders of treason.
[3] Many of these fines were held in reserve against future ill behavior. They thus acted as a kind of probation system.

and violence: Edward IV by making personal judicial progresses through the countryside and by issuing special commissions of *oyer* and *terminer*,[4] Henry VII by relying rather more upon the justices of the peace and the common law courts. Most important of all, perhaps, Edward, by introducing a more effective supervision of the customs system and by reorganizing the administration of the royal lands on lines copied from the most up-to-date methods of private estate management, increased his normal revenues to the point where he almost achieved the contemporary ideal that the king "should live of his own" without burdening his subjects with demands for direct taxation except in cases of emergency. Financially, Henry followed where Edward led, with the same desirable results. The English monarchy had once again become an effective institution.

The New Aristocracy

This tragic sequence of political events, its later stages immutably fixed in the popular mind by the dramatic exaggerations of Shakespeare's tragedies, seems to support Bishop Stubbs's famous and oft-quoted condemnation: "Weak as is the fourteenth century the fifteenth is weaker still, more futile, more bloody, more immoral." The interpretation of social tendencies, also, until comparatively recently, seemed to support this pessimistic verdict founded on a melodramatic sequence of political events. Now we no longer see the Black Death as an unmitigated tragedy, for by breaking a Malthusian cycle of overpopulation it considerably improved the living standards of the surviving masses. Similarly, modern research has shown that the horrors of the Wars of the Roses have been greatly exaggerated: the campaigns of these so-called wars occupied only thirteen weeks in thirty-two years; the numbers engaged in battle were generally small; the damage inflicted on the civilian population was minute compared with the devastations of contemporary fighting in other parts of Europe.

Moreover, until recently historians have tended to compare fifteenth-century facts, particularly as revealed in *The Paston Letters*, with earlier legislation, and, as remarked earlier, they often confused the aspirations of legislation with achievement. The early publication of this voluminous collection of letters,[5] written by an East Anglian family between 1417 and 1506, and its premature interpretation by writers lacking comparable evidence for both the preceding and the following periods seemed to reveal a luridly violent society almost on the verge of collapse. Now, as historians investigate more and more of the records of the law courts over several centuries, the contrast with earlier and later periods is very much

---

[4] Commissions to hear and determine (judge) special classes of offenses.
[5] Partly published in 1787.

diminished. The chronic violence of the fifteenth century was probably no worse than that of earlier centuries, and similar conditions continued at least until near the end of the sixteenth century.

At the same time, beneath the superficial and horrible violence of politics, developments occurred which shaped many English institutions into forms which survived, with, of course, considerable modification of detail and emphasis, into the twentieth century. One of the most prominent but, as yet, least recognized changes lay in the composition and nature of the aristocracy and the House of Lords. The standard, traditional account of the nobility claims that they were an old aristocracy, warlike, turbulent, and unruly; that by the end of the fifteenth century they were a group of thugs as out-of-date politically as troglodytes or dinosaurs. Already "decimated" during the Wars of the Roses by violent death in battle or by suppression for treason under acts of attainder, what remained of them were ruthlessly depressed by Henry VII, who relied in government upon "new men" of middle-class origin.

Unfortunately, this orthodox theory can only be described as a wild travesty of late medieval development. Henry VII and his descendants certainly relied on new men, but so had all his predecessors, and Henry's new men were far from being middle class in the way in which this term is most commonly used. Aristocracies, and the English aristocracy is no exception, have always deluded the general public with legends of their own antiquity. The English aristocracy as it existed in the later Middle Ages and in Tudor times had very little connection with Norman blood, with those who fought for William the Conqueror at Hastings, or even, as a group, with the major barons of Magna Carta. They were, in fact, a contemporary creation. The great period of change during which the new aristocracy emerged was the late thirteenth and the early fourteenth centuries, and the years between the mid-fourteenth century and the end of the reign of Queen Elizabeth I (1558–1603) were a period of remarkable stability in its history. There was no real break either during the Wars of the Roses or with the change of dynasty in 1485.

By the reign of Edward I only a dozen or so earls still survived from an earlier Anglo-Norman and Angevin aristocracy. Immediately below them in the social hierarchy were about 3,000 or more landowners with incomes exceeding £20 a year. This minority group of the population (probably about 2 percent) bore the burden of local government. Historians have traditionally called this group the "gentry," a term which would be better abandoned in favor of "minor nobility," for these same historians have endowed the word "gentry" with distinctly middle-class overtones, whereas in their source of income (the land) and their habits and ways of life they were much closer to the now emerging titled peerage than to the urban merchant classes. Many Elizabethan writers, like Thomas Wilson, in fact, called this class the "minor nobility."

The few earls apart, before the end of the thirteenth century none of this landowning class, however rich individual members of it might be, bore any special marks or titles of distinction. Then, to widen the basis of support for the monarchy, Edward I, as well as summoning representatives to Parliament, sent individual invitations to a number of other rich and powerful men besides the surviving earls—and to such men the title "baron"[6] was gradually applied. Thus some of the greater estate owners split off from the ranks of the minor nobility in general through the distinction of an individual summons to Parliament. Though wealth was essential, the choice of candidates for the higher rank was otherwise, to say the least, haphazard in the extreme, and for many years the distinction was certainly not hereditary. Edward I summoned forty-one such barons in November 1295, as many as seventy-four in February 1297, and there was a wide range of between forty-six and a hundred in the Parliaments of his later years. The king obviously felt that the option of choice was his, and he used it freely according to the needs of the moment to obtain the presence in Parliament of a fairly large group of people who would be useful for the particular affairs which he had in hand. For example, the names of the fifty-three barons whom he summoned to the August Parliament of 1295 seem to have been taken from an earlier list or lists concerned with summonses for military service to the Welsh and Scottish wars. Over two-thirds of them held lands near the Welsh and Scottish borders. They were certainly not representative of the greater English landowners as a whole, either in numbers, wealth, or position.

Within a very few years the king lost this element of choice. Just as the political tensions of Edward II's reign consolidated the position of the Commons in Parliament, so during the same years the new peerage began to close its ranks. From about 1312 the lists began to stabilize, a process well-established by 1330, and from then onward the majority of barons summoned held the estates, or part of the estates, of those who had been earlier distinguished in the same way. By the 1340s the new peerage, including the earls,[7] had settled down to between fifty and sixty members. The titled aristocracy, the greater aristocracy, had become a small group which remained fairly constant at this figure until a great "inflation of honors" took place under the early Stuarts, when between 1603 and 1640 the number of peers increased from 60 to about 150.

[6] "Baron" is a confusing term, as it had earlier been applied to men who held a certain quantity of land (roughly twenty knight's fees or more) of the king as feudal tenants-in-chief and who possessed certain special privileges. There was, of course, some continuity of individual families between the two groups, but the coincidence of name has led many historians to formulate a nonexistent general connection between earlier feudal barons and later parliamentary barons. Some parliamentary barons, in fact, held only a very small proportion of their estates as tenants-in-chief.
[7] Superior and more varied titles were introduced later, some in imitation of foreign usage: duke, 1337; marquess, 1386; viscount, 1437.

This stability in numbers was not, however, matched by stability in blood. Turnover within the privileged group was always rapid. The appalling rate of infant mortality saw that every twenty-five years or so one-quarter of these families died out in the male line. The total numbers of the peerage were maintained only by continuous new creations, so that a considerable proportion of the lords were always "new men." We should, however, be very careful in distinguishing the meaning of this term. In spite of snobbish gibes against some men newly elevated to the peerage, it most emphatically does not mean middle-class men, let alone men of low birth "raised from the dust." It means, as it had meant from the beginning, men promoted from a pool of rich, untitled landowners, whose sources of income, habits, and ways of life were indistinguishable from those of the existing peerage, to whom, in any case, many of the "new men" were closely related by blood and marriage.

By the mid-fourteenth century, if not earlier, such men were no longer primarily the tough, brutal warriors of the Anglo-Norman period. In spite of the prominent part which some of them took in the Hundred Years War, they were more a nobility of service than a military nobility—a nobility of service in much the same manner as Tudor aristocrats are wrongly supposed to have been for the first time. All the essential changes in the habits and functions of the group had already taken place, and the later fifteenth and sixteenth centuries saw only some changes in tone. With foreign warfare after 1453 limited more or less to sporadic, isolated campaigns, their character and interests became more and more civilian. Even in the fourteenth century the criterion for entry to the charmed circle was not only, or even primarily, military service: that was more likely to be rewarded by election to the Order of the Garter than by elevation to a barony. John Tiptoft, for example, who had been a servant of Henry IV, both before and after the revolution of 1399, acted as soldier, administrator, speaker of the House of Commons, and royal counselor before he became a baron in 1426, and his son, with no military record at all, was promoted to an earldom in 1449.

Nor can we any longer claim that the Yorkists and the early Tudors tried to suppress the nobility. They tried to keep them under firm control, certainly, but suppression—No! If these kings had really wished to suppress the nobility, they could easily have allowed it to die out through natural causes. Like their predecessors, however, they kept it going through new creations. In fact, from the 1440s the kings of England quite deliberately created new peers to support the throne and its occupants during periods of political tension. Great nobles remained prominent in all vital affairs: in raising troops for the now infrequent royal forays overseas, for the suppression of the occasional dangerous revolt at home, and, above all, in the continuous discipline of maintaining order in the countryside. In all these matters the kings of England had no effective alternative to the services provided by the peerage and their connections and dependents among the minor nobility: concentrations of interest around local great men, the system of clientage and mutual interdependence generally known as "bastard feudalism."

Justices of the Peace

All this was still notably true in spite of the almost contemporary emergence of the justices of the peace—an institution which ever since has formed the local basis of the English judicial system. From the late twelfth century local knights had, from time to time, been made keepers of the peace; that is, they were given powers to enquire into crime but not to give judgments. During the early fourteenth century the Commons, strongly supported by some of the peers, pressed for the grant of judicial powers to such men, a demand for their transformation from keepers to justices of the peace. The government and professional lawyers were, on the whole, opposed to the introduction of such a system, preferring the use of extraordinary, special commissions composed of magnates and lawyers. By 1368, after a long series of experiments and false starts, the Commons had their way, and every county received its commission of justices of the peace with jurisdiction over felonies and trespasses, weights and measures, labor laws, and, as time went on, a good many other matters. By the early seventeenth century Englishmen looked upon this system as one of unique efficiency, the like of which was unknown anywhere else in Europe. At the time of its inception, however, it was far less effective than it afterwards became (and still remains), for its efficiency was limited by inadequate control from the center and inadequate policing of the countryside. No medieval government ever possessed the resources to provide both sufficient control and sufficient support for the system. At the time it did not, and could not, replace the aristocracy and bastard feudalism in the maintenance of order in the countryside. It was a decent and, as time went on, an increasingly effective supplement to their activities, but for two centuries or more it hardly replaced them.

English Becomes the National Language

Ultimately, the development of a common language was essential to the development of national unity. Anglo-Saxon England had been unique in Europe for its use of the vernacular in government. The Norman Conquest, replacing it with Latin for administration and with French as the spoken tongue of the small upper class, reduced English for at least two centuries to the degraded status of a "kitchen language." The extent of its submergence should not, however, be exaggerated. After all, estate officials needed to be trilingual: they had to keep their accounts in Latin and report to their employers in French, but they could hardly conduct business with peasantry, tenants, and serfs in any language other than English. Although the literature of the aristocracy was written in French, a considerable volume of oral poetry in English must have survived amongst the common people, and the more conscientious of the higher clergy thought it their duty to preach in the vernacular. Stephen Langton, Archbishop of Canterbury at the time of Magna Carta, lectured in Latin, wrote some of his letters in French, and delivered some of his sermons in English.

English began to gain ground in the thirteenth century, made rapid strides in the fourteenth, completely ousted French in the fifteenth, but not until the Tudor period did it become a vehicle capable of intellectual expression at the highest level.

During the thirteenth century, the sheriffs read Magna Carta in English for the benefit of those attending the shire courts who could not understand Latin and French. King Henry III had one of his proclamations translated, and Robert of Gloucester's verse history of the barons' war appeared in English.

Although there is no doubt about the ultimate transformation, conflicting evidence makes the chronology of change in the fourteenth century somewhat uncertain. Many years later, and possibly, therefore, not very reliably, the chronicler Froissart (1347–1410), claimed that when the Hundred Years War began Parliament ordered all lords, knights, and townsmen to teach their children French as it would be useful in the war, a statement which, taken at its face value, surely indicates that the language had been rapidly losing ground. On the other hand, some historians have claimed that the anti-French emotions which the war aroused stimulated the use of English. In 1348 a schoolmaster made his pupils translate their Latin into English rather than French, and this practice soon became general. In 1363 the chancellor opened Parliament in English for the first time; the previous year the government had commanded lawyers to conduct their pleadings in English. With the conservatism typical of their profession, they ignored the order for generations, so that as late as the early seventeenth century a legal reporter wrote such gems of French as "il ject un brickbat a le dit defendent que narrowly mist."[8] By 1385 John of Trevisa (1362–1412), who translated both a history of England from French and an encyclopedia from Latin into English, said "nowadays boys know no more French than their left heel." "English-French," by this time, had become a mere provincial dialect, for Geoffrey Chaucer gently satirized the prioress in the Prologue to *The Canterbury Tales* (c.1388–93):

[8] Although legal reports, then and later, were still made in Anglo-French, it is still not clear when this ceased to be the spoken language of the courts—probably some time in the sixteenth century.

And French she spak ful faire and fetisly,
After the scole of Stratford atte Bowe
For French of Paris was to hir unknowe.

Edward III could speak English, and it may have been Richard II's mother tongue. In 1399 the estates of the realm renounced their fealty to Richard, and Henry IV set out his claim to the Crown in English, whereas in 1327 the rebels had conducted all proceedings against Edward II in French. As far back as 1383 the City of London had issued a proclamation in English. Henry V used it for propaganda purposes, sending dispatches to the city announcing his successes in the French wars. The Brewers' Company, thereupon noting that "our most excellent King hath procured the common idiom to be recommended by the exercise of writing and the greater part of the lords and commons have begun to make their matters to be noted down in our mother tongue," ordered that in future their own ordinances should be written in English.

The brewers' declaration, however, somewhat anticipated the progress of English in administration, although from this time onward its progress was steady and cumulatively rapid. While formal, stereotyped, routine documents, such as royal grants of land and offices, and estate accounts continued to be issued in Latin, in less formal documents such as privy seal writs, signet letters, and petitions to the chancellor, the contents of which called for more subtle, more spontaneous modes of expression and less standardized formulae, Latin and French increasingly gave way to English. From the late 1430s the king had to appoint a special French secretary as he could no longer rely upon a knowledge of the language in all his staff. Perhaps the surest sign of progress lies in the evidence of the Rolls of Parliament. All through the fifteenth century formalized and routine statements, such as those of the opening and closing of the assembly and the appointment of the speaker, were generally recorded in Latin, but French yielded to English for description of the proceedings. The printed edition of the Roll for 1403–04 contains roughly 41 columns in French, none in English; by 1467–68 there was no single complete column of French but 112 in English.

The progress and development of English as the national language, however, depended upon two things: the development of a standard form (one dialect had to establish its mastery over many) and the greater extension of its powers of expression. Chaucer, Trevisa, and, as late as the 1490s, William Caxton all made the point that the people of the North and those of the South could hardly understand each others' dialects, but Trevisa also remarked that Midlanders could understand both. As a result of extensive immigration from the East Midlands into London, the East Midland dialect became that of the city, the court, the government, and the royal justices of assize, who helped to carry it across England. Caxton's employment of East

Midland for his printed books helped to spread this particular form, and, finally its use, after the Reformation, in the English Bible completed its triumph as the standard form, the basis of modern English.

If, by the end of the fourteenth century, English was gaining ground, its utility was distinctly limited. It was still a comparatively underdeveloped language whose capacities for expression varied tremendously for different purposes. In the genius of Chaucer and Langland it had achieved, in different ways, a brilliant maturity in poetry, although most of Chaucer's fifteenth-century successors are disappointing by comparison with the master. Prose writing, however, was another matter entirely: a coherent, fluid prose style always takes longer to develop, and, in some ways, fifteenth-century conditions were unpropitious.

The fifteenth century saw an increase in the facilities for education, but little or no improvement in its content. There were more schools but little or no change in the curriculum. Literacy had long ceased to be a clerical monopoly. It may be that as much as 30 percent of the population could read and write, perhaps as much as 40 percent by 1530. Yet outside the universities the level of teaching was inevitably low, for, before the invention of printing, it was only the exceptional schoolmaster who could afford to buy books. Fifteenth-century schools produced an increasing number of laymen, many of them in quite humble circumstances, who could draft, in both Latin and English, the formal documents needed in their businesses and some who could write of daily events more or less graphically reproducing the speech of everyday life. An ability in the laborious drafting of simple business documents is, however, far removed from fluency in vivid narrative or the lucid expression of abstract ideas. With the brilliant exception of Sir Thomas Malory's *Le Morte d'Arthur*, achievement in prose was not high. During the fifteenth century, a number of vernacular chronicles replaced the earlier Latin and French chronicles of the city of London. Significant as they are as evidence of a trend, only a most intense chauvinism could claim much for them either as literature or as sources of historical evidence. Their thin narratives, poverty-stricken vocabulary, and myopic vision compare very poorly with the accomplished writing of earlier monastic Latin chronicles; their mostly anonymous authors delighted in the credulous reproduction of rumors and long, immensely detailed descriptions of pageants and ceremonies which modern readers find insufferably tedious. In another field, during the second quarter of the century Bishop Reginald Pecock (d. 1460–61?) was the first to attempt the writing of highly technical theological treatises in English. The results show that such attempts were still hardly feasible in a language that had so far failed to develop many abstract nouns.

It took two or three generations longer before men like Sir Thomas More (1475–1535), trained in the new humanistic Latin culture derived from Italy, developed an effective prose style capable of flowing narrative and the subtle expression of ideas. As Professor Denys Hay has pointed out, More and others of his generation who wrote a vigorous, expressive English prose had all been trained in this new Latin scholarship. Although English steadily gained ground, it took two centuries before authors could finally overcome the limitations which a somewhat underdeveloped vocabulary and prose structure imposed upon them. The increased educational opportunities of the fifteenth century helped to create a wider reading public amongst the laity, but it was not until the early sixteenth century that both a highly developed language and a lay intelligentsia emerged.

England at the Beginning of the Sixteenth Century

The developments which we have traced in government, in economic and in social life provided the basis for modern society. Nevertheless, England at the beginning of the sixteenth century was far from being a modern state. In spite of the expansion of the cloth industry, it was still an agrarian community with a very low degree of productivity and all the rigid limitations on prosperity, living standards, and governmental activity which logically follow from comparative poverty. Not least amongst these inevitable restrictions were the narrow activities of the central government, which were almost confined to the maintenance of defense and public order. Its activities were, on the whole, negative, disciplinary, and repressive. The more positive aspects of modern government, such as responsibility for education and social welfare (or charity, as it was then known and practiced), still fell to the Church and to what private benevolence, strongly connected with religious devotion and religious duty, felt inclined to provide. Consequently, the provision of such services was distinctly haphazard, organized more according to the personal inclination of well-to-do benefactors and the chance distribution of wealth than according to regional and local need.

Within these initial limitations, English institutions functioned only imperfectly: there was always a wide, although as time went on a gradually diminishing, gap between theory and practice. The means at the government's command were always more exiguous than its functions. Government lacked adequate physical coercive sanctions. The armies which fought the Hundred Years War were incredibly small, the largest of them hardly more than 15,000 men, and were raised for particular expeditions, not on a permanent basis. Apart from these forces there were a few garrisons, by far the largest of them stationed at Calais, and Calais' peacetime quota of 800 men (raised to 1,000 in wartime) was always a dreadful financial strain on the Exchequer. Edward IV and Henry VII had a royal bodyguard of about 200 men. These small establishments apart, there was no money to pay either a standing army or a police force—or a civil service of more than minute proportions. This was so because Englishmen regarded direct taxation as an abnormal expedient to be demanded only in emergencies, in time of war. In normal circumstances, as we have said, his subjects expected the king to "live of his own," that is, to live mainly on the proceeds of his landed estates and the customs. So because the royal income was so limited, so were the functions which the king and his few paid servants could directly perform.

Therefore, although the king enjoyed a freedom in deciding matters of high policy almost unknown to heads of state today, in the executive sense he could not govern alone. That reliance upon, that cooperation with the rich and the great, so notable in Anglo-Saxon times, was hardly less notable under the early Tudors. Government was still largely government by the rich, a function of property. People fully recognized that this was the case and they did not resent it. On the contrary, there is a good deal of evidence that they welcomed it. They felt that men already rich were least likely to oppress the people by corruption. Statute after statute on the Rolls of Parliament implies, or even explicitly states, that higher standards of honesty and fairness were to be expected from the well-endowed. Poor men had greater temptation to use office as a means of enriching themselves.

By modern standards, the government and its servants lacked even the most elementary information. They worked in an ignorance which it takes a major effort of the imagination to grasp. They had no idea even of the numbers of the population. In 1371 the government, for taxation purposes, estimated the number of parishes at 40,000. The figure was the wildest of wild guesses, for there were only about 8,600. Expecting an invasion from Ireland, Henry VII had to send a special messenger to find out whether the Cheshire ports were capable of accommodating large ships. Even the judges worked under the most appalling difficulties. English common law was case law, based on decisions from individual cases, but unfortunately it did not develop logically from case to case. At the end of the thirteenth century there was a really horrible confusion of legal decisions and precedents, the almost unavoidable consequence of ignorance due to lack of communication in the governmental machine. The judges were simply ignorant of many decisions or simply forgot them. The haphazard memory of particular decisions and rulings, therefore, came to make up a good part of the common law. Even when the law was statute law, things were often no better. Judges, still relying upon fallible memory, heard cases without volumes of the statutes at hand. Although conditions may have become somewhat better during the fourteenth and fifteenth centuries, it was not until Edward IV took advantage of the introduction of printing to begin an edition of the statutes (to be followed by their sessional publication under Richard III) that a steady improvement came about.

The revived monarchy of the Yorkists and Henry VII, no less than the

English monarchy of the high Middle Ages, suffered all these limitations. It was not the strong, almost modern, monarchy that some historians have claimed, certainly not, after 1845, the "Tudor Despotism" of many generations of historical textbooks. Even by the European standards of its own day, its income and its resources were small: less than an eighth of those of the kings of France and less than a tenth of those of the Hapsburg emperor. England was definitely one of the second-class powers of the day. Edward IV and Henry VII kept their heads above water and paid their way because they were unadventurous and wisely abandoned the expensive dreams of European conquest, which had proved so disastrous financially and politically earlier in the fifteenth century. The monarchy's fundamental lack of resources would soon be revealed again when Henry VIII once more revived an aggressive European foreign policy. For the time, however, both Edward IV and Henry VII succeeded because they cut their coats according to the cloth available: limiting both aggressive instincts and expenditure, they successfully, and fairly cheaply, maintained what the majority of their subjects above all things desired, a fair measure of internal tranquility.

Select Bibliography

The standard reference works for this period are the relevant volumes in the Oxford History of England Series: R. G. Collingwood and J. N. L. Myers, *Roman Britain and the English Settlements* (1937); Sir Frank Stenton, *Anglo-Saxon England, c. 550–1087* (2nd ed., 1947); A. L. Poole, *From Domesday Book to Magna Carta, 1087–1216* (2nd ed., 1958); Sir Maurice Powicke, *The Thirteenth Century, 1216–1307* (2nd ed., 1962); M. Mc-Kisack, *The Fourteenth Century, 1307–1399* (1959); E. F. Jacob, *The Fifteenth Century, 1399–1485* (1961). A good short introduction to the subject is Helen Cam, *England Before Elizabeth* (1950). A. L. Poole, ed., *Medieval England*, 2 vols. (1958) is a most readable series of essays on (among other things) landscape, architecture, trade and towns, costume, education, books, and recreations.

Introduction

C. Cipolla, *The Economic History of World Population* (Penguin Books, 1960) sets the preindustrial scene and discusses its profound differences from that of the modern technological age. P. Laslett, *The World We Have Lost* (2nd ed., 1971) gives a fascinating discussion of society, community, and the family in the preindustrial age. Most of his evidence is taken from the seventeenth century, but his conclusions have almost equal validity for earlier periods.

Chapter One

M. Charlesworth, ed., *The Heritage of Early Britain* (1952) contains essays by various authors. The first four chapters cover this period in an interesting and lively way. G. P. Welch, *Britannia: The Roman Conquest and Occupation of Britain* (1963) and P. H. Blair, *Roman Britain and Early England* (1963) are good introductions to the subject. S. Frere, *Britannia* (1967), much longer and more detailed, is one of the best modern books on the subject. M. and C. H. B. Quennell, *Every-day Life in Roman Britain* (1925) and A. Birley, *Life in Roman Britain* (1964) deal very well with economic, social, and cultural life. A. L. F. Rivet, *Town and Country in Roman Britain* (rev. ed., 1964) and *The Roman Villa in Britain* (1969) deal very well with these subjects; the second of these books is much the more detailed. B. Cunliffe, *Fishbourne* (1971) is a lavishly illustrated account of discoveries following the recent excavations of the greatest house yet discovered in

Roman Britain. D. Divine, *Hadrian's Wall* (1969) is a popular and readable account of the northern defenses.

J. and C. Hawkes, *Prehistoric Britain* (1953) is the best short introduction to this subject.

Chapters Two and Three

Good introductory books are G. O. Sayles, *The Medieval Foundations of England* (1961), chs. 1–14, and D. Whitelock, *The Beginnings of English Society* (Penguin Books, repr., 1965) (the introductions in the same author's book of documents, *English Historical Documents, c. 500–1042* [1955], are well worth studying); P. H. Blair, *An Introduction to Anglo-Saxon England* (1956) and *Roman Britain and Early England* (1963); R. I. Page, *Life in Anglo-Saxon England* (1970). R. H. Hodgkin, *A History of the Anglo-Saxons* (3rd ed., 1952) is detailed and magnificently illustrated. S. B. Chrimes, *An Introduction to the Administrative History of Medieval England* (2nd ed., 1952). Chapter 1 is a brief and sound introduction to the governmental system.

Some students may find the following original authorities interesting: Bede, *Ecclesiastical History of the English People*, ed. B. Colgrave and R. A. B. Mynors (1969); *The Anglo-Saxon Chronicle: A Revised Translation*, ed. D. Whitelock, with D. C. Douglas and S. I. Tucker (1961); F. L. Attenborough, *The Laws of the Earliest English Kings* (1922); A. J. Robertson, *The Laws of the English Kings from Edmund to Henry I* (1925); W. H. Stevenson, *Asser's Life of King Alfred*, ed. D. Whitelock (1959).

On more specialized topics, the following deal with the early conquests: G. J. Copley, *The Conquest of Wessex in the Sixth Century* (1954) and R. V. Lennard, "The Character of the Anglo-Saxon Conquests," in *History*, XVIII (1933). The best picture of Germanic society on the eve of the migrations is in H. M. Chadwick, *The Heroic Age* (1912).

The following deal with ecclesiastical affairs and the influence of Anglo-Saxon England in Europe: M. Deansley, *Augustine of Canterbury* (1964); J. Godfrey, *The Church in Anglo-Saxon England* (1962); N. W. Bryant, "Bede of Jarrow," in *History Today*, XIX, no. 6 (1969); S. J. Crawford, *Anglo-Saxon Influence on Western Christendom, 600–800* (1933); W. Levison, *England and the Continent in the Eighth Century* (1946); E. S. Duckett, *Anglo-Saxon Saints and Scholars* (1947) and *Alcuin* (1951).

On administration, see W. Morris, *The Medieval English Sheriff to 1300* (1927); pp. 1–39 deal with that important officer. On the boroughs, see C. Stephenson, *Borough and Town: A Study of Urban Origins in England* (1933), pp. 47–72, and R. R. Darlington, "The Early History of English Towns," in *History*, XXIII (1938). J. Tait, *The Medieval English Borough* (1936) is complicated and rather difficult but is the classic exposition. V. H. Galbraith discusses charters and writs in *Studies in the Public Records* (1948), ch. 2; also see F. M. Stenton, *Latin Charters of the Anglo-Saxon Period* (1955).

G. Jones, *A History of the Vikings* (1968) is good although somewhat detailed.

For the monarchy in general and particular kings, see H. R. Loyn, "The King and the Structure of Society in Late Anglo-Saxon England," in *History*, XLII (1957); C. N. Brooke, *The Saxon and Norman Kings* (1963); B. A. Lees, *Alfred the Great, The Great Truth Teller* (1915), together with a new approach toward the Alfredian period in R. H. C. Davis, "Alfred the Great: Propaganda and Truth," in *History*, LVI (1971); L. M. Larson, *Canute the Great* (1912); and F. Barlow, *Edward the Confessor* (1970).

Chapter Four

The following general accounts are highly recommended: D. M. Stenton, *English Society in the Early Middle Ages* (4th ed.; Penguin Books, 1967) and F. Barlow, *The Feudal Kingdom of England, 1042–1216* (2nd ed., 1963).

The best studies on the Norman background to the Conquest and Norman influence in Europe generally are C. H. Haskins, *The Normans in European History* (1915; re-issued, 1959), the classic work on the subject, and more up-to-date, D. C. Douglas, *The Norman Achievement* (1969). T. Baker, *The Normans* (1966) gives a more popular but sound account. In a short pamphlet, J. Le Patourel, *The Normans* (Hastings and Bexhill Historical Association, Eng., 1966) deals with the feudal situation in Normandy before the Conquest.

There are numerous studies of the Norman Conquest itself. Among the most recent are H. R. Loyn, *The Norman Conquest* (1965); R. Allan Brown, *The Normans and the Norman Conquest* (1969); D. J. R. Matthew, *The Norman Conquest* (1966); R. H. C. Davis, "The Norman Conquest," in *History*, LI (1966).

On the very controversial topic of the introduction of feudalism into England, see J. H. Round, "The Introduction of Knight Service into England," in *Feudal England* (repr., 1964); F. M. Stenton, *The First Century of English Feudalism* (2nd ed., 1963); C. W. Hollister, *The Military Organisation of Norman England* (1965); and S. Harvey, "The Knight and the Knight's Fee in England," in *Past and Present*, no. 49 (1970).

On the nature and development of Anglo-Norman government, the following are most useful: R. W. Southern, "The Place of Henry I in English History," in *Proceedings of the British Academy*, XLVIII (1962); J. O. Prestwick, "War and Finance in the Anglo-Norman State," in *Transactions of the Royal Historical Society*, 5th ser., vol. IV (1954); and R. H. C. Davis, "What Happened in Stephen's Reign, 1135–1154," in *History*, XLIV (1964). V. H. Galbraith discusses the making of the great Domesday survey in *Studies in the Public Records* (1948), ch. 4, and in a much more extended and detailed form in *The Making of Domesday Book* (1961). H. M. Cam, *The Hundred and the Hundred Rolls* (1930), especially pt. one, is a good introduction to local government. Good biographies are D. C. Douglas, *William the Conqueror* (1964); F. Barlow, *William I and the Norman Conquest* (1965); R. H. C. Davis, *King Stephen* (1967); and H. A. Cronne, *The Reign of Stephen, 1135–1154: Anarchy in England* (1970). See also C. N. Brooke, *The Saxon and Norman Kings* (1963).

Chapter Five

The best general introductions are again Stenton, *English Society, op. cit.,* and Barlow, *The Feudal Kingdom, op. cit.* Good accounts are also found in D. M. Stenton, "Henry II," in the *Cambridge Medieval History*, V (1926), 554–91, and F. M. Powicke, "England: Richard I and John," in *ibid.*, VI (1929), 218–51, and in the introductions to D. Douglas and G. W. Greenaway, *English Historical Documents, 1042–1189* (1953).

The most important features of this period are (1) the development of government and (2) the reaction of the propertied classes toward its harsher features culminating in the revolt which led to Magna Carta under King John. (1) can be studied in W. Stubbs, *Historical Introductions to the Rolls Series*, ed. A. Hassall (1902), pp. 89–181, and in S. B. Chrimes, *An Introduction to the Administrative History of England* (1953)—Chapter 3 deals with the development of government in general. The classic study of the development of law is F. Pollock and F. W. Maitland, *The History of English Law Before the Time of Edward I* (2nd ed., 1898). A good up-to-date summary on the same subject is T. F. T. Plucknett, *A Concise History of the Common Law* (5th ed., 1956). A short pamphlet by R. B. Pugh, *Itinerant Justices in English History* (1967), gives an admirably clear account of an essential but complicated topic. An interesting, and at times amusing, account of the judicial duel is V. H. Galbraith's "The Death of a Champion (1287)," in *Studies in Medieval History Presented to F. M. Powicke*, eds. R. W. Hunt, W. A. Pantin, and R. W. Southern (1948), pp. 283–95. Much the best short account of the development of the Exchequer is to be found in the introduction by C. Johnson to the *Pipe Roll of Richard I* (Pipe Roll Society, N.S.I., 1925). C. Johnson has also published a new edition of the *Dialogus de scaccario* together with a translation and an introduction in *Dialogus de Scaccario* (Medieval Classics Series, 1950). On the development of the public records and "written government," see V. H. Galbraith, *The Public Records* (1952), ch. 2. Morris, *The Medieval Sheriff to 1300, op. cit.*, chs. 2 and 3,

should again be consulted for the activities of that official, while H. M. Cam, *Liberties and Communities in Medieval England* (1944; repr., 1963), ch. 3, throws valuable light on the social origin of the sheriffs. (2) A. L. Poole discusses the effect of government on various social classes in a lively way in *Obligations of Society in the XII and XIII Centuries* (1946). J. E. A. Jolliffe, in *Angevin Kingship* (rev. ed., 1963), discusses, with a wealth of detail, the interesting theory that government was a struggle between the inertia of a custom-ridden community and the innovating will of powerful kings. J. C. Holt, *Magna Carta* (1969) is now the standard work on this topic. The same author's pamphlet *King John* (Historical Association London, 1963) is useful. F. M. Powicke, *Stephen Langton* (1928) discusses the great archbishop's role in the making of the charter.

D. Knowles, *Thomas Becket* (1970) is a distinguished study. *The Becket Controversy*, ed. T. M. Jones (1970), gives extracts from both original sources and modern authors. The following biographies are also worth study: C. H. Walker, *Eleanor of Aquitaine* (1950); J. T. Appleby, *England Without Richard, 1189–1199* (1965); C. R. Cheney, *Hubert Walter* (1967).

Chapter Six

The most readable short economic history is Sir John Clapham, *A Concise Economic History of England From the Earliest Times to 1750* (1949). S. Pollard and D. W. Crossley in *The Wealth of Britain* (1968), chs. 1–3, offer a brief up-to-date account of medieval and Tudor economic development. E. Lipson, *Economic History of England*, vol. I (11th ed., 1956), remains the best and most reliable standard account. H. C. Darby, *Historical Geography of England Before 1800*

(1936) is a most useful volume of essays. W. G. Hoskins, *The Making of the English Landscape* (1955), chs. 1–4, describes the evolution of the English countryside from earliest times to the end of the Middle Ages. M. W. Beresford and J. K. St. Joseph in *Medieval England: An Aerial Survey* (1958) provide a volume with fascinating photographs and plans and discussions of the development of individual places and sites.

On the countryside, peasant life,

and agrarian organization, H. S. Bennett, *Life on the English Manor* (1937) is the standard work on village and manorial life. G. G. Coulton, *The Medieval Village* (1925) is still worth reading. G. C. Homans, *English Villagers of the Thirteenth Century* (1941) is somewhat more specialized; C. S. and S. C. Orwin, *The Open Fields* (1967) analyzes the organization of the farm and fields. J. Z. Titow, *English Rural Society, 1200–1350* (Historical Problems, Studies and Documents Series, no. 4, 1969) discusses sources, population, and standards of living among the rural population of this period. A. R. Bridbury, *Economic Growth: England in the Later Middle Ages* (1962) discusses the same problems for the fifteenth century, although this work has a wider scope, dealing also with trade and industry. Both can profitably be read with E. Miller's article, "The English Economy in the Thirteenth Century," in *Past and Present*, no. 28 (1964), which covers a much wider period than its title indicates. M. M. Postan, "The Chronology of Labour Services," in *Transactions of the Royal Historical Society*, 4th ser., vol. XX (1937), analyzes the various phases of labor services. R. H. Hilton, "Peasant Movements in England Before 1381," in *Economic History Review*, 2nd ser., vol. II (1949; repr.); E. M. Carus-Wilson, ed., *Essays in Economic History*, II (1969), deals with peasant unrest and the decline of serfdom. The standard account of the peasants' revolt of 1381 is C. Oman, *The Great Revolt of 1381*, ed. E. B. Fryde (1969). See also B. Wilkinson, "The Peasants' Revolt of 1381," in *Speculum*, XV (1940). Interesting accounts of individual estates are to be found in E. Miller, *The Abbey and Bishopric of Ely* (1951); R. A. L. Smith, *Canterbury Cathedral Priory* (1943); H. P. R. Finberg, *Tavistock Abbey* (1951). These, all studies of ecclesiastical estates, have been chosen because they cover fairly long periods

of time. There are, unfortunately, no comparable studies of lay estates. E. A. Kosminsky, "Services and Money Rents in the Thirteenth Century," in *Economic History Review*, V (1934–35), draws an interesting comparison between the methods of exploitation on large and small estates.

On trade in general, see L. F. Salzman, *English Trade in the Middle Ages* (1931).

On England's major export commodities, wool and woolen cloth, see E. E. Power, *The Medieval English Wool Trade* (1941) and E. M. Carus-Wilson, "An Industrial Revolution of the Thirteenth Century," "The English Cloth Industry in the Late Twelfth and Early Thirteenth Centuries," and "Trends in the Exports of English Woollens in the Fourteenth Century," in *Economic History Review*, XI (1941), XIV (1944), and 2nd ser., vol. III (1950). These articles are also reprinted in the same author's *Medieval Merchant Venturers* (1954). The story is continued for the fifteenth century in E. Power and M. M. Postan, *Studies in English Trade in the Fifteenth Century* (1933).

J. F. W. Hill, *Medieval Lincoln* (1948) is a good study of a particular town. W. Robertson, Jr., *Chaucer's London* (1968) is a mine of information, if somewhat discursive. S. L. Thrupp, *The Merchant Class of Medieval London* (1948) is a good analysis of the social structure of the fourteenth- and fifteenth-century city.

On gilds, see G. Unwin, *The Gilds and Companies of London* (1908), especially chs. 1–12.

L. F. Salzman, *Building in England down to 1540* (1952) is interesting and sound, and M. W. Barley, *The English Farmhouse and Cottage* (1961), pt. one, and M. Wood, *The English Medieval House* (1965) deal with housing.

M. W. Labarge, *A Baronial Household in the Thirteenth Century* (1965) gives an interesting account of aristocratic life.

Chapter Seven

For general accounts, see again D. M. Stenton, *English Society in the Early Middle Ages, 1066–1307* (4th ed., Penguin Books, 1967).

On the development of government and baronial opposition and revolt under Henry III, see E. F. Jacob, "Henry III," in *Cambridge Medieval History*, VI (1929), 252–83. A brilliant, but very detailed, account is F. M. Powicke, *King Henry III and the Lord Edward*, 2 vols. (1947), especially chs. 1–4, 7–8, 10–13. More specialized studies are found in E. F. Jacob, "What Were the 'Provisions of Oxford,' " in *History*, IX (1924–25), and in R. F. Treharne, *The Baronial Plan of Reform, 1258–1263* (1932) and "The Significance of the Baronial Reform Movement, 1258–1267," in *Transactions of the Royal Historical Society*, 4th ser., vol. XXV (1942).

There is no good up-to-date general account of Edward I, but G. Templeman, "Edward I and the Historians," in *Cambridge Historical Journal*, X (1950), gives a good summary of different views put forward by successive historians. H. M. Cam, "The Quo Warranto Proceedings Under Edward I," in *Liberties and Communities in Medieval England* (1944, 1963) and T. F. T. Plucknett in *The Legislation of Edward I* (1949) and *Edward I and Criminal Law* (1960) deal with Edward I's legislation. Both books at times become somewhat technical but are well worth study. Interesting verdicts on Edward's reign and character are given in Powicke, *King Henry III and the Lord Edward, op. cit.*, ch. 16, and D. W. Sutherland, *Quo Warranto Proceedings in the Reign of Edward I, 1278–1294* (1963), ch. 8.

Literature on Parliament is enormous and only a very small selection can be mentioned here. On early development, the best general account (although in need of considerable revision) is still A. F. Pollard, *The Evolution of Parliament* (2nd ed., 1926; new ed., 1964). *Early English Parliaments: High Courts, Royal Councils, or Representative Assemblies*, ed. G. P. Bodet (Problems in European Civilization Series, 1967), gives a useful introduction to the topic and interesting extracts from the works of recognized authorities. See also J. F. Baldwin, *The King's Council in England During the Middle Ages* (1913), pp. 1–68, and F. Thompson, *A Short History of Parliament, 1295–1642* (1953). Also E. Miller's pamphlet, *The Origins of Parliament* (Historical Association, 1960). T. F. T. Plucknett, "Parliament," in *The English Government at Work, 1327–1336*, shows how Parliament was functioning in the early fourteenth century. An interesting essay on origins and comparisons with parliaments elsewhere is H. G. Richardson, "The Origins of Parliament," in *Transactions of the Royal Historical Society*, 4th ser., vol. XI (1928), reprinted in *Essays in Medieval History*, ed. R. W. Southern (1968). On representation, see M. McKisack, *The Parliamentary Representation of the English Boroughs During the Middle Ages* (1932; repr., 1962). *Historical Studies of the English Parliament*, ed. E. B. Fryde and E. Miller, vol. I (1970), contains a useful introduction and reprints of articles originally published in learned journals—in particular, those by J. E. A. Jolliffe and F. W. Maitland (stressing the importance of justice in the origins of Parliament), J. G. Edwards (on taxation and the composition of the Commons), and H. M. Cam (on the representative system and the origins of legislation). See also J. G. Edward's pamphlet, *The Commons in Medieval English Parliaments* (1958). J. E. Powell and K. Wallis, *The House of Lords in the Middle Ages* (1968), the only recent book on this topic, although it contains information and interpretations not found elsewhere, is, in form, more a work of reference than an analysis.

Chapter Eight

Good introductions to the subject of this chapter are A. R. Myers, *England in the Later Middle Ages* (2nd ed., 1965) and G. Holmes, *The Later Middle Ages, 1275–1485* (1962). Myers is fuller on political events and the arts, while Holmes is particularly good in discussing the institutions of government. J. R. Lander, *Conflict and Stability in Fifteenth Century England* (1969) discusses in particular (as well as brief accounts of politics) economic, religious, and social developments. The same author's *The Wars of the Roses* (1965, 1966) is a book of documents with a valuable introduction on the effects of the wars. A. R. Myers, *English Historical Documents, 1327–1485* (1969) is a mine of fascinating information and contains long sections of valuable introduction to the various classes of documents. F. R. H. Du-Boulay, *An Age of Ambition* (1970) is very good on social and family relationships, education, religion, and economic affairs.

M. Hastings, *The Court of Common Pleas in the Fifteenth Century* (1947) and C. Ogilvie, *The King's Government and the Common Law, 1471–1641* (1958) provide good accounts of the state of the law and the legal system.

On the political side, the following are informative: T. F. Tout, *The Place of Edward II in English History* (2nd ed., 1936); S. Armitage-Smith, *John of Gaunt* (1911; repr., New York, 1965); and A. Steel, *Richard II* (1941). M. McKisack, "Edward III and the Historians," in *History*, XIV (1960), gives an interesting interpretation. The following deal with Henry V and the conquest of Normandy: R. A. Newhall, *The English Conquest of Normandy* (1924) and *Muster and Review: A Problem of English Military Administration, 1420–1440* (1940). For Edward IV and Henry VII, the following may be consulted: J. R. Lander, "Edward IV: The Modern Legend and a Revision," in *History*, XLI (1956); B.

P. Wolffe, *Yorkist and Early Tudor Government, 1461–1509* (Historical Association Aids for Teachers Series, no. 12, 1966); R. Lockyer, *Henry VII* (1968); and R. L. Storey, *The Reign of Henry VII* (1968). Indispensable for the financial revival of the monarchy is B. P. Wolffe, *The Crown Lands, 1461–1536* (1970). The following deal with the revival of monarchical power: J. G. Bellamy, "Justice Under the Yorkist Kings," in *American Journal of Legal History*, IX (1965), and C. G. Bayne and W. H. Dunham, Jr., *Select Cases in the Council of Henry VII*, (Selden Society, LXXV, 1958). A. R. Myers, "Richard III and Historical Tradition," in *History*, LIII (1968), 181–202, gives a fascinating account of this monarch's reputation.

The following works are good on the nobility: Lander, *Conflict and Stability, op. cit.* ch. 7; G. A. Holmes, *The Estates of the Higher Nobility in Fourteenth Century England* (1957); K. B. McFarlane, "Bastard Feudalism," in the *Bulletin of the Institute of Historical Research*, XX (1943–45), 161–80, and "The Wars of the Roses," in the *Proceedings of the British Academy*, I (1965); W. H. Dunham, Jr., "Lord Hastings' Indentured Retainers, 1461–1483," in *Transactions of the Connecticut Academy of Arts and Science*, vol. XXXIX (1955).

On the use of French and the development of the English language, see H. Suggett, "The Use of French in England in the Later Middle Ages," in *Transactions of the Royal Historical Society*, 4th ser., vol. XXVIII (1946), reprinted in *Essays in Medieval History*, ed. R. W. Southern (1968), and R. W. Chambers, *On the Continuity of English Prose From Alfred to More and his School* (Early English Text Society, 1932). N. F. Blake, *Caxton and His World* (1969) gives a level-headed account of Caxton's quality as a printer and of the influence of translations upon the development of English.

Kings and Queens of England

Important Kings Before the Norman Conquest

Bretwealdas
c.	477–491	Aelle, King of the West Saxons
c.	560–584	Caelwin, King of the West Saxons
	584–616	Aethelbert, King of Kent
c.	600–616	Raedwald, King of East Anglia
	616–632	Edwin, King of Northumbria
	633–641	Oswald, King of Northumbria
	654–670	Oswiu, King of Northumbria

King of Mercia
758–796   Offa

Kings of the West Saxons
802–839   Egbert
866–871   Aethelraed
871–899   Alfred
899–925   Edward the Elder

(Beginning in Egbert's time the West Saxon kings exercised authority over most of southern England, and Edward the Elder and his successors exercised a varying amount of control over the Scandinavian kingdoms in the north. In 954 this control became permanent and from then onward the kings of the West Saxons ruled all England.)

Rulers of England
959–975   Edgar the Peaceable
979–1016   Aethelraed the Redeless
1016–1035   Cnut
1042–1066   Edward the Confessor
1066   Harold Godwinson

Normans
1066–1087   William I
1087–1100   William II
1100–1135   Henry I
1135–1154   Stephen

Angevins-Plantagenets
1154–1189   Henry II

1189–1199	Richard I
1199–1216	John
1216–1272	Henry III
1272–1307	Edward I
1307–1327	Edward II
1327–1377	Edward III
1377–1399	Richard II

Lancastrians

1399–1413	Henry IV
1413–1422	Henry V
1422–1461	Henry VI

Yorkists

1461–1483	Edward IV
1483	Edward V
1483–1485	Richard III

Tudors

1485–1509	Henry VII
1509–1547	Henry VIII
1547–1553	Edward VI
1553–1558	Mary (I)
1558–1603	Elizabeth I

Stuarts

1603–1625	James I
1625–1649	Charles I
1649–1660	Commonwealth and Protectorate
1660–1685	Charles II
1685–1688	James II
1688–1702	William III and Mary (II)
1702–1714	Anne

Hanoverians

1714–1727	George I
1727–1760	George II
1760–1820	George III
1820–1830	George IV
1830–1837	William IV
1837–1901	Victoria
1901–1910	Edward VII
1910–1936	George V
1936	Edward VIII
1936–1952	George VI
1952–	Elizabeth II

Index

180

A 3
B 4
C 5
D 6
E 7
F 8
G 9
H 0
I 1
J